SIMPLY PLANTS

SIMPLY PLANTS

FEEL-GOOD VEGAN RECIPES TO NOURISH THE BODY AND SOUL

SADIA BADIEI

Creator of Pick Up Limes

Clarkson Potter/Publishers

New York

Clarkson Potter/Publishers
An imprint of the
Crown Publishing Group
A division of
Penguin Random House LLC
1745 Broadway
New York, NY 10019
clarksonpotter.com
penguinrandomhouse.com

Library of Congress Cataloging-in-Publication Data
Names: Badiei, Sadia [author]
Title: Simply plants: feel-good vegan recipes to nourish the body and soul / Sadia Badiei, creator of Pick Up Limes.
Description: New York: Clarkson Potter/Publishers, [2026] | Includes index.
Identifiers: LCCN 2025034020 (print) LCCN 2025034021 (ebook) | ISBN 9798217033843 hardcover | ISBN 9798217033850 ebook
Subjects: LCSH: Vegan cooking LCGFT: Cookbooks
Classification: LCC TX837 .B216 2026 (print) | LCC TX837 (ebook) | DDC 641.5/6362—dc23/eng/20251118
LC record available at https://lccn.loc.gov/2025034020
LC ebook record available at https://lccn.loc.gov/2025034021

ISBN: 979-8-217-03384-3
Ebook ISBN: 979-8-217-03385-0

Editor: Jennifer Sit
Editorial assistant: Elaine Hennig
Designer: Yasmeen Bandoo
Art director: Stephanie Huntwork
Production designer: Christina Self
Production editor: Liana Faughnan
Production: Phil Leung
Compositor: Barbara Peragine
Photography and recipe development team: Suzy Borchert, Andrea Wetzels, Sanja Prejac, María Fuentenebro, Robin de Rozario, and Sadia Badiei
Copy editor: Kate Slate
Proofreaders: Eldes Tran, Sigi Nacson, and Miriam Taveras
Indexer: Elizabeth Parson
Publicist: Kristin Casemore
Marketer: Emily Hotaling

Manufactured in China

10 9 8 7 6 5 4 3 2 1

First Edition

The authorized representative in the EU for product safety and compliance is Penguin Random House Ireland, Morrison Chambers, 32 Nassau Street, Dublin D02 YH68, Ireland, https://eu-contact.penguin.ie.

TO THE PICK UP LIMES COMMUNITY:

This book exists because of you.
Thank you for cooking with me,
again and again.

Contents

Welcome!

Welcome to *Simply Plants,* the very first Pick Up Limes cookbook!

What started as a creative outlet in my little kitchen has since grown into something far beyond what I ever imagined—a global community of millions who share a love for simple, nourishing plant-based food. Whether you've been following along since the early YouTube days or just stumbled on this book today, I'm so glad you're here.

When I was working as a dietitian, I came to realize how much pressure people put on themselves when it came to food. I saw how well-meaning advice about "eating healthy" often spiraled into overwhelming food rules: Cut out sugar, avoid oil, go low-carb, eat only "clean" foods. Even many vegan cookbooks encouraged these kinds of restrictions. And while the intentions are often rooted in a genuine desire to support health, in my experience, these rules can become unsustainable. Over time, the pendulum tends to swing in the other direction and can lead to feelings of disappointment, inadequacy, and an unhealthy relationship with food.

That's why at Pick Up Limes, we take a different approach: *no extremes, no guilt—simply plants.* Instead of cutting things out, we focus on adding foods that are simple to make, satisfying to eat, and easy to keep coming back to. Food is there to support our health, yes, but it should also bring joy without adding pressure. When it feels good and fits into your life, it's easier to stick with. And when you do eat more plants, good things ripple outward: for your health, for animals, for the planet. *Slow and steady wins the race.*

In this book you'll find over one hundred recipes carefully created to nourish both your **cells** and your **soul** (our motto! More on this on page 17). From veggie-packed meals to decadent desserts and everything in between, there's a recipe here for every appetite.

My hope is that this book feels like a steady, supportive presence in your kitchen. That it invites ease rather than overwhelms, and encourages a kinder way of eating: rooted in nourishment, free from pressure, and full of flavor.

I can't wait for you to dive in.

With love,

Creator of Pick Up Limes

The Kitchen: My Happy Place

I've spent years thinking about how food makes us feel.

Not just how it tastes, or how nutritious it is, but how it *feels*.

The way it comforts you on hard days. The way it connects you to people you love. The way one bite can carry you somewhere familiar, even if you're half a world away.

That feeling is what this book is about: the reminder that food can nourish us in more ways than one.

Food hasn't always felt this way for me. For a long time, it was something I rushed through, overanalyzed, or tried to control instead of enjoy. The kitchen, for me, went from being a place of indifference to a place of pressure. Allow me to explain. . . .

Growing up, I was lucky to have parents who cooked often. I remember the patience they brought to the kitchen. In a world that often rushes, they cooked slowly. Pots simmered for hours, bread rose in its own time, and the air filled with the scents of our Afghan and Iranian roots—warm cardamom, cumin, turmeric, and dried herbs. I only wish I had appreciated it more back then.

As a teenager, I didn't really *get* the beauty of home cooking. Still, I was drawn to food. I worked in restaurants throughout high school and into early adulthood. Not always glamorous jobs, but definitely formative ones. I learned to move fast in a busy Italian kitchen, plate mezze in a cozy Lebanese restaurant, and, ironically, serve steaks and all-you-can-eat ribs at a bustling grill house. I didn't know it then, but those experiences would shape how I thought about food: how flavors balance, how dishes come together, how much care goes into every plate. But when it came to cooking at home, I didn't see it as something I *wanted* to do. If I had to make something for myself, it was usually a grilled cheese sandwich or instant noodles.

That didn't change much when I moved into university dorms. With a cafeteria downstairs and a demanding class schedule, I lived on convenience foods and energy drinks. Of all things, I chose to major in dietetics—not because I cared much about nutrition, but because I thought it might be a stepping stone into medical school. If I didn't get in right away, at least I'd still be able to work in a hospital.

But slowly, studying nutrition began to rewire how I thought about food. I started cooking more. Not because I had to, but because I *wanted* to. What started as curiosity turned into full-blown fascination. I signed up for two university courses on the science of cooking: one focused on theory, while the other was hands-on. We'd prepare the same dish multiple ways, then break down why each one turned out the way it did.

At night, I'd lie in bed thinking of odd flavor pairings I hadn't yet dared to try. Could cinnamon work in soup? Would tahini and jam be a terrible idea? I'd wake up hungry—for food, and for answers.

That same year, with no housing available on campus, my sister offered me a room in her home. She wouldn't let me pay rent, so I repaid her the best way I knew how: with food. I cooked whatever I could, from breakfasts and dinners to little snacks to tuck into lunch bags. It was my way of saying thank you, and an excuse to keep experimenting.

Then came the turning point: an unexpected scene in *The Walking Dead,* of all things—a post-apocalyptic show where humans are trying to survive a zombie outbreak. I'll spare the gory details, but one particular episode drew a haunting parallel between how animals are treated and how humans

were portrayed. I decided, then and there, that I didn't want to eat animals anymore. I wanted to eat more plants.

Like many people starting something new, I turned to YouTube for guidance. But most of what I found promoted an ultra "clean" way of eating: no oil, no sugar, no processed foods of any kind. I gave it a go. Some things worked, others didn't, but I noticed that meals became more about restriction than enjoyment. Food started to feel like a checklist of what I could and couldn't have.

I was eating to be *perfect,* not to *feel good.*

At some point, I realized I had lost the joy that first drew me to food. That realization changed everything.

It made me ask myself: *Why am I relying on strangers online when I've been trained to understand nutrition?* I had just completed a degree in dietetics. I knew how to read studies, question trends, and look beyond the sensational headlines. And what I was seeing online didn't always match the evidence. In fact, a lot of it was harmful—fueling fear and perfectionism disguised as "health."

Look, food shouldn't make you anxious. It shouldn't make you feel guilty or see yourself as "good" or "bad" because of what you ate. It should make you *feel good*—physically, emotionally, and ethically.

So I started over.

I cooked with curiosity instead of judgment. I began creating meals that were balanced, practical, and nourishing.

Around that time, my sister and a close friend encouraged me to share what I was learning. To document the recipes I was testing, the tips I was uncovering, the little moments of joy I was finding in the kitchen. But I was hesitant. I didn't see myself as someone who belonged in front of a camera. And part of me worried: What would my colleagues think? The doctors and dietitians I worked with? The word "influencer" made me cringe, and the idea of putting myself out there felt overwhelming. The seed had been planted, but I just wasn't quite ready to water it.

So how did I go from second-guessing myself in front of the camera to sharing recipes with millions of people—and now to this cookbook you're holding in your hands?

Here's the short version: I met a boy.

He's Dutch. I'm Canadian. We met while backpacking through Thailand and figured it would never work. But love has a funny way of pulling distant things closer. Just ten months after we met, I left my job at a hospital in Canada and moved to the Netherlands to live with Robin, who had just started his PhD in engineering.

Some people might find that impulsive, but I thought the idea had its charm. I packed my bags and made the leap, mostly for love, and partly for a fresh start. I realized that being in a new country might offer a sense of anonymity, and that made the idea of posting videos online a little less intimidating. The distance gave me space. Space to try things. To experiment. To build something new.

Slowly, I began filming nutrition and recipe videos from our tiny forty-square-meter (about four hundred square feet) apartment. I launched a little website called Pick Up Limes and posted my first

YouTube videos. Each morning, Robin would head off to the university, and I'd begin my daily ritual of rearranging our apartment furniture: moving the dining table into the living room where the lighting was best for filming, and pushing the couch back into the kitchen to accommodate it—even if it meant the fridge door was nearly impossible to open. Our tiny bedroom had a singular shelf, not designated for our clothes but instead piled high with bowls, plates, and various food photography props.

It was all very makeshift. I felt unsure most of the time, but also wildly inspired.

The growth was slow at first . . . until it wasn't. Six months in, everything changed. We jumped from 10,000 to 100,000 subscribers in three weeks. A few weeks later, we hit a million.

On that very day, two other life-changing things happened: I was granted a five-year visa to stay in the Netherlands, and I received an acceptance letter to medical school.

Suddenly, I was standing at a crossroads. I could return to Canada, leave behind the person I loved, and pursue the career I had spent years working toward. Or I could stay, take a chance on something new, and keep building this platform that was starting to feel like something meaningful.

In the end, I chose Pick Up Limes. And I chose love.

Since then, our YouTube community has grown to over four million subscribers, with more than a quarter of a billion views. We eventually outgrew our little apartment and moved into a more spacious studio and test kitchen. What started as a solo venture slowly grew into something much bigger.

When Robin finished his PhD, he joined full-time. With his background in engineering, he completely rebuilt our website, and created our mobile app from the ground up. Over time, we were lucky enough to welcome a small but mighty team—from fellow dietitians and recipe developers to photographers and videographers—all working behind the scenes to help bring Pick Up Limes to life.

Together, we carved out our mission: *to make plant-based living more accessible to everyone, everywhere.*

And as our little corner of the internet continued to grow, one question started popping up more than any other: *When are you coming out with a cookbook?* Truthfully, I wanted to wait until it felt right. I wanted this book to be the best it could possibly be. So over the years, as we tested and developed recipes for our website, I secretly set aside some of the ones that really stood out. These were the dishes that I and our team kept making on repeat in our own kitchens. Recipes that never failed to impress, and after nearly a decade of cooking and creating, I finally felt like the list of all-stars was complete.

This is our debut cookbook. It's a collection of the recipes we love the most. Most are brand new, but I've also included a few longtime fan favorites from our website and app, refreshed with new photos and, in some cases, small tweaks to make them even more approachable (so even if you recognize one, it might be worth giving it another go!). Consider this book the ultimate Pick Up Limes collection, with all my favorites gathered in one place.

I hope this book brings you joy in the kitchen. That it inspires meals that nourish both body and soul. That it helps you fall in love with cooking, and shows just how much you can do with simply plants. Nothing would make me happier.

Welcome to my kitchen. The room I used to avoid, and now build my days around. My happy place. My sanctuary.

Let's get cooking.

My Food Philosophy

"Nourish the cells & the soul."

Back when I was working in hospitals and clinics, I could really feel the tension around food. So many patients and clients seemed to carry this weight of judgment and anxiety with every meal. In today's world, with diet culture everywhere, it's easy to get caught up in chasing an unrealistic idea of health. We're bombarded with terms like "clean," "good," "bad," and "guilt-free," which only fuel these misguided beliefs about food.

When I started Pick Up Limes, my goal was to create a space that felt calm, welcoming, and kind. I didn't want food to feel like something to fear or obsess over. I wanted it to be something to enjoy and celebrate.

That's where our motto came from: *Nourish the cells and the soul.* Because to me, eating well isn't just about nutrition. It's also about comfort, connection, and joy.

When I say *nourishing the cells,* I'm talking about the bountiful, nutrient-dense foods nature gifts us: vibrant veggies, hearty grains, refreshing fruits, power-packed legumes, nuts, and seeds. Eating these foods makes us feel good and keeps our bodies strong and healthy.

But *nourishing the soul* goes deeper. It's the connection we have with food that goes beyond just eating. It's the stories a particular dish tells, the memories it evokes, and the comfort it brings on a tough day. It's the laughter shared over a family dinner, the warmth of a hot drink on a cold night, and the sheer joy of baking cookies *just because.* It's about the traditions passed down through generations, and the thrill of discovering a new cuisine. It's recognizing that food isn't only about nutrients or calories but about experiences, emotions, and the richness it adds to our lives. To truly nourish the soul is to understand that every bite carries with it a piece of history, a moment, and a feeling. Nourishing the soul is celebrating food as an act of love, an art, and a bridge that connects us to ourselves and the world around us.

This cookbook reflects that philosophy by showcasing a wide variety of dishes. Over the years, with a global audience tuning in, it's been fascinating to see how differently people respond to certain ingredients. Some say we use too much oil, others say not nearly enough. The same goes for salt and sugar. Everyone has their own preferences, shaped by culture, upbringing, and experience.

Personally, I feel I fall somewhere in the middle. I believe in balance. I try to use mostly whole-food ingredients, but I'm not afraid of a little oil, sugar, or anything else that adds flavor and enjoyment. If there's one thing my time in the restaurant world taught me, it's that these ingredients can bring a dish to life. And if that helps more people enjoy plant-based food, that's a win in my book.

I want this way of eating to be sustainable, and for me, that comes from flexibility, not purity. In a society so influenced by diet culture, it's easy for the pursuit of health to become an overwhelming preoccupation. But it doesn't have to be this way. We can eat in a way that supports our well-being and still make room for joy. We shouldn't be afraid to enjoy a decadent dessert or a dish that leans a little more indulgent. Whether it's a crisp, wholesome salad or a gooey slice of chocolate cake, everything has its place at the table.

I firmly believe no food should carry the label of "good" or "bad." That kind of thinking can mess with our relationship with food and steal the joy that comes with eating. Because at the end of the day, food isn't just fuel. It's something to be experienced, to be shared, and to be savored, for both the body and the soul.

Nutrition 101

Shortly after Robin and I met, we went on an absurdly long eight-hour hike. We were still getting to know each other, so the conversation moved in every direction. Somewhere along the way, he asked, "If there's one thing you could teach me about nutrition, what would it be?"

He came from an engineering background and said he didn't know much about nutrition, but was curious to learn. I remember feeling stumped. My mind raced with everything I'd learned. So much of it was tied to specific health conditions or required long explanations. How could I possibly narrow it down to *just one thing*?

After a pause, I shared the one tool I believed could help anyone, anywhere, make more nourishing meals without needing to overthink it: the plate method.

From that day on, I noticed him mentally checking his plate. Was there a source of protein? Did it have some grains and veggies? I was proud and reassured. It's a simple tool, but a powerful one. One that makes good nutrition feel more intuitive and doable.

The Plate Method

The plate method is a simple way to picture what a balanced plant-based meal can look like. With so much mixed messaging around nutrition, it's easy to feel unsure about how to get "enough" of everything. Traditional food guidelines often focus on counting portions and tracking numbers, and while some people find that helpful, most people find it confusing and hard to maintain. The plate method takes a different approach. It offers structure—just enough to guide your meals without being rigid. It's not a diet. There's nothing to count, track, or measure. It's simply a visual guide. A way to bring balance to meals without the stress.

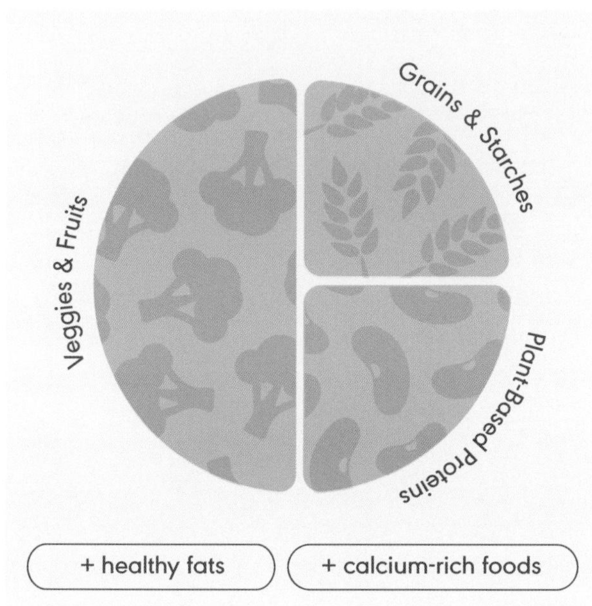

The Basic Breakdown

Here's the visual structure:

½ **of the plate:** vegetables and/or fruits
¼ **of the plate:** grains and/or starches
¼ **of the plate:** plant-based protein

And woven through or alongside the meal are **healthy fats** and **calcium-rich foods.**

A Closer Look at Each Section

VEGGIES AND FRUITS (½ OF THE PLATE)

Vegetables and fruits are packed with fiber, vitamins, minerals, antioxidants, and water, all of which are key players in everything from digestion to energy levels. The goal is variety. Eat the rainbow! Whether fresh, frozen, canned, or fermented, all forms count.

GRAINS AND STARCHES (¼ OF THE PLATE)

Grains and starches give us energy. Think rice, quinoa, pasta, millet, oats, bread, potatoes, and other root veggies. When possible, choosing whole grains (like brown rice or whole-grain bread) offers added fiber, B vitamins, and minerals, but all types of grains and starches can have a place, depending on what's available and what you enjoy.

PLANT-BASED PROTEINS (¼ OF THE PLATE)

Protein helps with fullness, blood sugar regulation, tissue repair, and more. In a plant-based diet, that might mean lentils, chickpeas, beans, tofu, tempeh, edamame, seitan, or even commercial meat alternatives. It's helpful to include a protein source in most meals, especially those meant to be more filling or long-lasting.

FATS AND CALCIUM-RICH FOODS (SUPPORTIVE SIDES)

Though not represented as a "slice" of the plate, healthy fats and calcium-fortified dairy alternatives round things out. Adding a spoonful of tahini, a drizzle of olive oil, or a handful of walnuts can make a meal more satisfying and help your body absorb fat-soluble nutrients.

Calcium-rich foods are also important, and while you don't need to include them in every meal like the main components of the plate, aim to enjoy them a couple of times throughout the day. This might look like 1 cup of calcium-fortified plant milk, ¾ cup of plant-based yogurt, or ½ cup of calcium-set tofu.

Why It Matters

Plant-based diets can be incredibly nourishing, but they're not automatically balanced. The plate method makes sure we're not leaning too heavily on one type of food. It reminds us that protein deserves a regular spot on the plate. That fat isn't something to avoid, but something to welcome. That calcium needs attention, even when dairy isn't in the picture. This breakdown helps make sure you're getting a variety of nutrients, like fiber, complex carbs, protein, vitamins, and minerals, without having to overthink it.

A NOTE ON THE WORD "DIET"

I've never loved the word "diet." When I say "plant-based diet," I don't mean it in the weight-loss sense, I mean it as a way of eating, a lifestyle. Some prefer to say "plant-based lifestyle," and that works, too. If you extend it beyond food, to avoiding animal products in clothing and other products, that's where the word "vegan" comes in. Whatever you call it, the heart of it is the same: making choices that are kind to our bodies, to animals, and to the planet.

Beyond the Plate

Some dishes, like soups, curries, wraps, or breakfast bowls, may not be as easy to portion visually. That's okay. The plate method still applies conceptually.

Let's say you're having a sandwich. You're probably already covering grains with the bread and protein with something like hummus or tofu. Could you add lettuce and tomato, or a side of fruit? Great! There's your produce. As a bonus, a handful of almonds or a glass of calcium-fortified plant milk on the side, and now you've hit every key area.

Or maybe dinner is a bowl of curry with lentils and rice. The legumes are your protein, the rice covers your starch. Can you stir in some greens or add a cucumber salad on the side? Maybe swirl in some coconut milk for fat or plant-based yogurt for calcium? Done.

It's less about needing to "get it right" and more about learning to spot what's missing and knowing how to fill the gap.

Not Every Meal Needs to Fit

It's worth saying (and *emphasizing*): The plate method is just a guide. It doesn't have to look perfect or be followed at every meal. Some meals won't check every box . . . and that's okay! Sometimes lunch is just toast with peanut butter, or dinner is soup and crackers. That's life. What matters more is the overall pattern. If you stay mindful of the general pattern, and include a variety of foods from each group across the day or week, things tend to balance out naturally.

That's the beauty of the plate method: It takes away the pressure. It brings nutrition back to basics, and brings a sense of calm and confidence into the kitchen.

And to me, that's exactly what good nutrition should feel like.

COOK ALONG WITH OUR APP

As a special gift for picking up this cookbook, you get free access to all the cookbook recipes in our mobile app, so that you can view them from anywhere online. We created this app to help you feel more supported in the kitchen with:

- A **step-by-step guide** for every recipe, with a photo for each step so you can follow along just as we did in our own kitchen.
- A detailed **nutrition breakdown of each recipe,** so that you can feel confident about the way you're nourishing yourself and your loved ones.
- **Allergen information** and ingredient swap suggestions to help you tailor meals to your (family's) needs.
- Access to our vibrant community chats, where **your questions are answered** by our team of chefs and dietitians.
- A **serving size scaler** that automatically adjusts the ingredients so you can cook for any party size you like.

To unlock your free access, scan the QR code and answer a few questions to verify your purchase. Then, create your own Pick Up Limes account and download the Pick Up Limes app from the App Store (iOS) or the Google Play Store (Android).

And if you like our app, consider trying the full version **7 days for free** to unlock thousands of **additional delicious plant-based recipes** and premium features that include: personalized meal planning, nutrition tracking, smart grocery shopping lists, and a space to save recipes and to create your own.

How to Succeed with Cooking

1. Follow first, freestyle later.

Growing up, I don't think I ever saw either of my parents use a measuring spoon. When I asked them for a recipe, they'd laugh and tell me to taste and adjust until it felt right. I admired their intuition, but when I tried cooking that way, I could never fully re-create their dishes. I learned that intuition comes after you've cooked something enough times to trust your judgment.

So here's my take: The first time you try a recipe, follow it as closely as possible. Especially when it comes to baking or unfamiliar dishes. There's been a lot of testing behind the scenes to make sure the recipes work. Once you get a feel for it, you'll know where you might want to add your own spin next time.

2. Read before you cook.

It takes just a minute, but it can save your dinner. Always read the recipe from start to finish before you begin. This one step can save you from realizing halfway through that you're missing an ingredient or needed to soak something in advance.

When you know what's coming, you can prep smarter and cook more efficiently without surprises and without scrambling.

3. Practice mise en place.

A fancy French term that basically means: Get everything ready before you start. Wash, chop, measure, and lay everything out so you're not sprinting to find the cinnamon while something burns on the stove.

4. Keep your knives sharp.

Few things make cooking more frustrating than a dull knife. Every time we stay in a vacation rental, I'm reminded how much harder it is to prep a meal when the knives can barely cut through a tomato. But more important, it's unsafe. Dull blades need more force and are more likely to slip, which increases the risk of cutting yourself. *Yikes!*

That's why it's worth sharpening your knives every once in a while. A simple honing tool goes a long way, and if you're not sure how, there are plenty of quick videos online. Alternatively, drop them off for a professional sharpening now and then. Trust me, future you will thank you.

5. Clean as you go.

This isn't glamorous advice, but it might be the most underrated tip of all. Keep a little bowl nearby for veggie scraps as you chop. Wipe the counter while things simmer. Quickly rinse or wash anything you're done using.

When things stay tidy as you go, cooking feels way less overwhelming. No mountain of dishes at the end, no mess staring at you while you eat. Just a little habit that makes the whole experience feel calmer and more enjoyable (and more likely that you'll want to cook again tomorrow).

6. Cook with your eyes (not the clock).

Cooking times are always just estimates. In our professional studio kitchen, we use an induction cooktop, while at home we have a gas stove, which tends to cook things much faster. The type of pan you use can also affect cooking times, depending on how well it conducts heat. So instead of relying only on the minutes listed in the directions, look for *visual cues*. A golden-brown crust, a bubbling sauce, or an onion that's golden: These are your best indicators. Use your senses to know when something's done.

7. Taste early, tweak late.

When I first started cooking, I'd only taste a dish once I sat down to eat it, and by then, it was too late to fix anything. These days, I taste as I go to make sure things are heading in the right direction. Is the sauce getting too thick? Add a splash of water. Are the veggies softening too quickly? Reduce the heat. A small taste can help you course-correct before it's too late.

That said, the most important time to adjust is at the very end. *That's when you can bring everything into balance.* Even when following a recipe exactly, results can vary. Veggies come in different sizes, spice blends differ between brands, tomatoes might be more acidic than expected, and garlic can range from mild to sharp. All of these can affect the final flavor.

That's why tasting before plating is *essential.* Need a lift at the end? A splash of acid (like lemon juice or vinegar), a sprinkle of salt, or a touch of heat can take a dish from good to great. And be generous with garnishes! A handful of herbs or a sprinkle of toasted seeds can add brightness, texture, and contrast.

8. Bake with precision.

Baking is a science. Even small variations in the weight of flour, sugar, or baking soda can change how something rises, how moist it is, or whether it holds together at all. In our test kitchen, we have several sets of measuring cups, and they all give different results. A "cup" of flour might be 120 grams in one and 160 grams in another (yep, that's a *huge* difference!). That kind of inconsistency makes it hard to get reliable results. This is why *I recommend using a digital scale.* It gives consistent results, speeds up the process, and cuts down on dishes. Just tare between the ingredients and carry on!

That said, if you don't have one, you can still get pretty close with the right technique. Don't scoop your cup directly into the container, as that packs the ingredient down. Instead, *spoon it in gently and level it off* with the back of a knife. And unless the recipe says to pack it (brown sugar being the classic exception), don't.

Bonus Baking Tips

- Avoid swapping ingredients unless you're confident they'll work.
- Once the flour goes in, mix just until combined to prevent a dense or tough texture. In other words, *don't overmix!*
- Try not to open the oven door too often, as it lets out heat and can interrupt the baking process. Turn the oven light on and look through the window instead to check on progress.

HEADS-UP: All recipes in this book were developed using conventional heat (top and bottom elements on, fan off). If your oven uses convection (fan-assisted) heat by default, be sure to switch off the fan, as it can cause food to cook too quickly and affect the final texture. If the fan cannot be turned off, reduce the temperature by 25°F / 20°C, and start checking for doneness 5 to 10 minutes earlier.

9. Check your spice stash.

Spices and dried herbs are small ingredients that do a lot of heavy lifting in plant-based cooking, but if they've been sitting around for years, they're probably not going to do your dishes any favors. It's not that you *can't* use old spices, it's just that they won't be nearly as potent, which means your meals won't be as flavorful as they could be.

When I first got into cooking, I got a little carried away at our local Asian supermarket. The selection was amazing, the prices were great, and I figured buying in bulk would be a smart move. I'd portion out small amounts into jars that lined my windowsill, and the rest of the big bags went into the pantry, some of which sat there untouched for ages (I'm talking years). Over time, the colors faded, the aromas dulled, and I later learned they lost much of their antioxidant power, too.

These days, I buy smaller amounts more often and keep them tucked away in a cool, dark place, and never by the stove or on a sunny shelf—no matter how pretty they look on display—as light and heat make them degrade even faster (lesson learned). So check your stash! If your spices are old, you can try using a little extra, or replace them with something fresher. So for the best results, buy in small batches and aim to use them within 6 months to 1 year.

BLOOM SPICES

Blooming your ground spices in a bit of oil (or a dry pan) wakes them up and brings out incredible depth. Hold off on adding liquids until you've completed this step. You'll see this done throughout the recipes in this book. It's a small step that makes a big difference.

10. Don't crowd the pan.

One of the simplest ways to level up your cooking is to give your food some room. When veggies, tofu, or anything else are piled on top of each other, they end up steaming in their own moisture rather than browning. So to maximize flavor and texture, spread everything out in a *single layer* so each piece makes contact with the hot surface, and let it sit (mostly) undisturbed so it can properly brown. If your pan's too small or you're working with a lot of ingredients, cook in batches.

The same principle applies to baking. When the oven is overcrowded or trays are overloaded, heat can't circulate properly. If you're baking cookies, for example, give them space. Use two trays, or better yet, bake one at a time. It takes a little longer, yes, but they come out evenly golden, crisp on the edges, soft in the center—everything a cookie should be.

How to Create Flavor

I'm pretty sure I use the word "flavor" more than any other word. It's what makes food exciting. It's what turns a simple bowl of rice and veggies into something you look forward to eating again tomorrow.

While good flavor might feel like magic, it's really just chemistry. When I'm cooking, there are six things I look out for to make a dish more flavorful: **Fat, Acid, Salt, Sweet, Spice,** and **Temperature**. Together, they form the backbone of nearly every great dish. Remember them with one simple word: **FASSST**. Once you get the hang of how they work together, you'll know exactly how to tweak a dish to make it shine.

Think FASSST!

Fat

Fat helps flavor stick to your tongue. That's because many of the compounds that give food its aroma and complexity dissolve in fat. Without it, those flavors can't spread across your palate in the same way. Fat also adds body and a sense of comfort. It makes soups velvety, dressings creamy, and roasted vegetables taste more satisfying. It balances acidity, softens heat, and gives dishes a rounded finish.

Food sources: avocado, olive oil, vegan mayo, tahini, peanut butter, nuts, seeds, coconut milk.

Application: olive oil drizzled over roasted veggies, coconut milk stirred into curries, tahini in sauces, and nuts or seeds sprinkled onto salads.

Acid

Acids stimulate the salivary glands and increase saliva production. This literally wakes up your mouth, making your taste buds more sensitive to the other flavor elements in a dish. Acid brings balance when a dish feels too rich (it cuts through heaviness) or too flat (it adds brightness).

Food sources: lemon, lime, vinegars (all kinds), pomegranate molasses, kimchi, tomatoes, yogurt.

Application: lemon juice squeezed over grain bowls, vinegar whisked into dressings, kimchi in fried rice, yogurt in sauces, and tomatoes in stews.

Salt

Salt enhances flavor in a few powerful ways. It boosts aroma, so what you smell better match what you taste. It also suppresses bitterness and brings out sweetness and umami. That's why salt can make chocolate taste richer and vegetables taste sweeter. On a biological level, sodium ions activate taste receptor cells that heighten your ability to perceive other flavors. In other words, a pinch of salt makes everything *pop*. For best results, season gradually and consistently throughout cooking. A well-salted dish doesn't taste salty . . . it just tastes better.

Food sources: salt, soy sauce, miso, olives, capers, vegan feta.

Application: salt in pasta water, soy sauce in stir-fries, miso in broths or dressings, olives in salads or wraps, and feta crumbled over roasted vegetables.

Sweet

Sweetness helps bring balance to a dish. It can take the sharp edge off acidity, temper spiciness, and soften bitterness. Roasted vegetables develop sweetness through caramelization, while syrups and fruits in salads can soften intense flavors.

Food sources: fruit (fresh, dried, pureed), caramelized onions, maple syrup, agave syrup, sugar.

Application: fruit on salads, dates blended into desserts, caramelized onions served on burgers, and maple syrup in vinaigrettes.

"BUT TRAINING OUR PALATES TO FORGET ABOUT SWEET TASTES IS MUCH HEALTHIER"

I get a comment like this almost anytime I talk about the power of sweetness in adding flavor. Our taste for sweetness is natural. Instead of cutting it out completely, it can be more helpful to shift where it comes from. Sometimes that means using fresh fruit, like in the Chickpea Waldorf Wraps (page 73) or Curried Potato Salad (page 109). Other times it's dried fruit, like raisins in the Eggplant Caponata & Hummus Wraps (page 70) or Coconut Biryani (page 209). Caramelized onions add natural sweetness, too, like in the Mujadara (page 210).

At the same time, I'm not afraid to add a bit of sugar or syrup when it brings the kind of balance whole foods sometimes can't achieve on their own. A small amount of agave cuts through the bitterness of tahini in the Golden Rice bowls (page 213). A touch of sweetness softens the acidity of tomatoes in the Simple Vegan "Butter Chicken" (page 218). In each case, sweetness isn't added for the sake of it, but rather is used with intention to enhance the overall flavor of the dish. That said, if your palate prefers less sweetness, you can absolutely scale back or leave it out. Always do what feels right to you.

Spice

Spice works by activating heat and pain receptors in the mouth. That little burn from chile peppers or sharp kick from mustard can make a dish feel more lively and energizing. Similarly to acid, it also increases saliva production, which helps carry flavor across your palate and makes the dish taste more intense. Not every dish needs spice, but when it's there, it adds energy and excitement.

Food sources: sriracha, gochujang, harissa, sambal, chili crisp, chiles, black pepper, mustard, ginger.

Application: chili crisp spooned over noodles, gochujang stirred into sauces, mustard in dressings, and grated ginger in soups or stir-fries.

Temperature

Heat changes food at a molecular level. It affects the texture, color, and especially the flavor of what you're cooking. Two main reactions explain how this happens: the Maillard reaction and caramelization. The **Maillard reaction** happens when heat causes proteins and sugars in food to react. This creates new flavor compounds and a browned, savory surface. You'll notice it in foods like toasted bread, roasted veggies, and crispy tofu. **Caramelization** happens when sugars break down under high heat. This reaction creates a range of flavors that are sweet, rich, and slightly bitter. It also gives food a deep golden color. You'll see this in caramelized onions, roasted sweet potatoes, or the crackly top of a crème brûlée. These reactions show how temperature affects flavor. Knowing how to use heat can transform a dish as much as the ingredients themselves.

Cooking techniques: roasting, searing, caramelizing, simmering, browning.

Application: roasting cauliflower until golden, simmering stews until thick and rich, searing tofu until crisp, or caramelizing onions until sweet and jammy.

QUICK FLAVOR FIXES

TOO BLAND?

Start with salt or soy sauce. Then try acid like lemon juice or vinegar.

TOO SALTY?

Add more unsalted ingredients like rice or potato. Then try acid, followed by something sweet or creamy like coconut milk or yogurt.

TOO SOUR?

Sweetness is most effective! Add a pinch of sugar, or maple or agave syrup. If needed, follow with fat (like olive oil or tahini) or a bit of starch (like rice or potato).

TOO SPICY?

Creamy and cooling ingredients work best: Use coconut milk, yogurt, avocado, or nut butter.

TOO BITTER?

Sweetness helps most. Fat or acid can help round things out, too.

TOO SWEET?

Start with acid like citrus juice or vinegar. A small pinch of salt can also help.

TOO OILY OR HEAVY?

Add acid to cut through richness. Then try fresh herbs or crunchy raw vegetables or fruit to refresh and lighten the dish.

Getting to Know Your Ingredients

One thing I've learned in a plant-based kitchen is that ingredients don't always behave the same across different brands. A can of coconut milk might be rich and creamy from one brand and thin and watery from another. Nut butters might pour out like liquid or need serious stirring. Even vegan butter, cream cheese, and plant milks can vary quite a bit depending on the brand or what they're made from, like soy, coconut, or nuts.

If a recipe turns out a little differently than expected, it doesn't mean you've done something wrong. It might just be the ingredients doing their thing. Over time, you'll get to know what you like best and which brands work well in certain recipes. Until then, consider this chapter your guide to navigating some of the most nuanced plant-based ingredients.

Pantry Staples

Coconut Cream

Coconut cream is the thick layer that forms at the top of full-fat coconut milk when chilled. Some brands sell it separately, but if not, refrigerate your can of coconut milk and scoop it from the top. The amount of coconut fat separation can vary significantly between brands. If you don't get much separation, try a different brand for better results.

Dutch-Process Cocoa Powder

This type of cocoa is alkalized, which makes it less acidic and smoother in flavor than natural cocoa. It's our go-to for baked goods that need a mellow, rich chocolate taste.

Nutritional Yeast

Oh, the vegan's magical fairy flakes. Also known as nooch, nutritional yeast is a savory seasoning that adds an umami, subtle cheesy flavor to many dishes. But not all flakes are created equal. Flake size can vary, which affects both volume and strength of flavor. Coarser flakes might weigh around 40 grams per cup, while finer ones can weigh closer to 80 grams. So if a recipe calls for 2 tablespoons, the intensity might end up stronger or milder depending on the kind you're using. Give it a taste and adjust to your liking.

Oils

When I say "vegetable oil," use any neutral-flavored oil you like, such as canola, sunflower, avocado, etc. If I call for "olive oil" in a recipe for cooking on the stovetop, it's usually **refined olive oil** that can withstand higher temperatures. I'll specify **extra-virgin olive oil** specifically when it's used raw, as in dressings. If you see coconut oil in a recipe, I'm always referring to the **refined coconut oil**—which is the one without the coconut smell or taste.

Peanut Butter

I always use natural peanut butter with no added sugars or oils, but like coconut milk, the consistency can vary a lot between brands. Some are thick and scoopable, while others pour out like syrup. That can affect the texture of sauces, so adjust the thickness as needed by adding more peanut butter if the sauce is too thin or more liquid if it's too thick.

Plant-Based Milks

My go-to plant milk for most things is **soy milk**. It's one of the few options with a solid protein content, offering 8 to 9 grams per cup, which is similar to the amount found in dairy milk. This makes it especially useful in both cooking and baking. For savory cooking, if you're allergic to soy or not a fan, **almond milk** is the next best choice. It has a mild, neutral flavor that works well in most recipes. **Oat milk** is another popular option, but it's naturally a bit sweet, even when unsweetened. That subtle sweetness can be lovely in smoothies, breakfasts, or coffee, but it's not ideal for savory dishes.

In baking, protein plays a key role in building structure and flavor. Take vegan buttermilk, for example. When you combine soy milk with vinegar, the acid reacts with the protein and causes it to curdle. Almond or oat milk won't do the same, as they contain little to no protein. If you need a soy-free alternative for baking, **pea milk** is your best bet. It has a similar protein content to soy milk. While it can be a little harder to find and a bit more expensive, it's worth considering when structure matters.

ALL ABOUT SOY

There's a lot of fear around soy, both for health and environmental reasons. Many early health concerns came from animal studies or small trials that used very high doses of isolated compounds (far more than people would ever get from food). But overall, human research consistently shows that moderate soy intake is safe as part of a balanced and healthful diet. Large reviews have found no evidence that soy foods harm hormones, thyroid function, or men's health. On the contrary, studies point to potential benefits, especially for heart health. If you're concerned about pesticides or GMOs, organic soy milk is a simple fix, since organic standards restrict the use of genetically modified ingredients. And environmentally speaking, while soy farming does play a role in deforestation, only about 6 percent is used for human consumption, while the vast majority of that soy—over 75 percent—is grown to feed livestock. Eating plant-based actually helps reduce that demand.

Salt

All the recipes in this book use **fine sea salt**. It's dense and finely ground, which makes it more concentrated and noticeably saltier than lighter, flakier salts, such as kosher or coarse sea salt. Its clean, neutral flavor and ability to dissolve easily also make it especially reliable in both cooking and baking.

At home, though, I often use **iodized table salt**. It's a simple and consistent way to help support iodine intake, which is especially important on a plant-based diet. Iodine is essential for thyroid health, and while seaweed is a natural source, most of us don't eat it regularly enough to rely on it. Iodized salt offers a simple and consistent way to help meet those needs.

In chef circles, iodized salt is often avoided because it can leave a slightly metallic aftertaste in delicate dishes. I get that. Still, there's a reason it was introduced in the first place: Many people were (and still are) falling short on iodine. For those who don't regularly consume seaweed or take a supplement, iodized salt can help fill the gap. And the amount needed is small—a little goes a long way.

HEADS-UP: Salt tends to get a bad reputation, but that's mostly because of the large amounts used in processed foods like chips, instant noodles, and packaged snacks. Ironically, the salt in those foods is usually *not* iodized. One of the most dependable ways to get iodine is from the salt you use at home.

If you prefer another type of salt, that's totally fine. Just keep in mind that not all salts are created equal. Salt types vary in crystal size and density, so if you're swapping one for another, you may need to adjust the amount to taste.

As a rough guide:

1 Teaspoon Fine Sea Salt ≈

- 1 teaspoon iodized table salt
- 1¼ teaspoons Morton kosher salt
- 1¾ teaspoons Diamond Crystal kosher salt
- 1¾ to 2 teaspoons coarse sea salt

Tahini

Tahini comes in both raw and toasted varieties. **I prefer toasted tahini** for its deeper, nuttier flavor. Like nut butters, the texture can vary a lot from brand to brand: Some are thick and scoopable, while others are thin and runny. This can change the consistency of sauces or dressings, so feel free to adjust as needed to get the texture you like.

Fresh Ingredients

Herbs

I love herbs for the way they instantly brighten up a dish. You'll see them all throughout this book—blended into pestos, stuffed into salad rolls, or scattered over pastas. I measure them as "lightly packed," meaning I press them into the measuring cup just enough to fit snugly without crushing them. For those who like precision, I've included gram amounts, too, when larger volumes are used so you can weigh them out at home.

At the end of the day, herbs make everything taste better. If you ask me, don't err on the side of caution—err on the side of abundance.

Lemons & Limes

I usually don't give exact lemon or lime juice measurements in cooking recipes because it rarely needs to be that precise. Plus, there's nothing more annoying than trying to squeeze a lemon with one hand while holding out a measuring spoon with the other and hoping it doesn't spill everywhere. That said, I know some people prefer a bit more guidance. So based on my experience, here's what you can typically expect:

- 1 lemon or lime = about **2 tablespoons** juice
- ½ lemon or lime = about **1 tablespoon** juice

Keep in mind, the actual amount can vary quite a bit depending on the fruit's size, variety, and ripeness. Some large or extra-ripe lemons can yield up to **¼ cup** (4 tablespoons). I'm a huge acid lover, so in my kitchen, there's almost no such thing as too much lemon or lime. But if you're more sensitive to acidity, it's always better to start with less—you can add more to taste later.

HEADS-UP: Baking is a different story. In baked goods, acidity affects texture and rise, so in those cases, I do include exact measurements to keep the results consistent.

Tempeh

For the best flavor, go for the freshest tempeh you can find. It has a subtle nuttiness when it's fresh, but can taste sour or bitter if it's been sitting on the shelf too long. We've found that shops with high turnover usually carry the best tempeh. If you're unsure, give it a sniff before using it. Fresh tempeh should smell mild and earthy, not overly sharp or off-putting.

HOW TO PRESS TOFU

Pressing tofu simply means removing excess water so that the tofu can better soak up flavor, brown more easily, and hold its shape when cooked.

OPTION 1: TOFU PRESS

A tofu press is a small kitchen tool designed to hold the tofu block firmly in place while applying steady pressure. Most presses have adjustable screws or spring-loaded plates, and they're easy to use, clean, and store. Just place the block inside, tighten the press, and let it sit for about 10 minutes (or longer if you want!). Once pressed, pat the tofu dry before using.

OPTION 2: DIY WITH HOUSEHOLD ITEMS

No tofu press? No problem. Wrap the block in a clean kitchen towel or a few layers of paper towel, place it between two plates, and weight the top plate down with something heavy like a pot, pan, or book. Let it sit for 10 minutes, then pat dry before cooking.

OPTION 3: QUICK PRESS BY HAND

If I'm honest, I don't always have the patience to press tofu properly. When I'm in a rush, I just hold the block over the sink and gently squeeze it between my hands for a minute or two. The key is to apply light, even pressure so the tofu doesn't crumble apart. You won't remove as much moisture as with a full press, but it still helps and is better than nothing.

OPTION 4: BUY EXTRA-FIRM TOFU

Some supermarkets carry **extra-firm or super firm tofu.** These kinds have already been pressed during production, so they're really dense and don't hold much water. If you can get your hands on one, you can skip the pressing step entirely. Just pat it dry and carry on.

That said, it's not always easy to find. Since it's not available at every store, most recipes in this book call for regular firm tofu and suggest pressing it yourself.

Tofu

Tofu is one of the most versatile plant-based proteins. I get that it can seem plain or even a little boring at first, but that's kind of the magic. It's like a blank canvas: mild and neutral on its own, but it soaks up the flavors of whatever you cook it with. Marinate it, fry it, toss it into stir-fries . . . once you find your groove with it, you'll see just how much it can do.

Throughout this cookbook, you'll see I suggest pressing your tofu. Sometimes it's noted directly in the recipe and sometimes not—because in a few cases, it's not essential.

Vegan Butter, Cream Cheese, and Feta

These vary a lot depending on what they're made from. Some are coconut-based; others use cashews, almonds, or tofu. That can affect both the flavor and texture of the final dish, especially in baked goods. We test our recipes using the **Violife brand** (which is coconut-based) and recommend it when you can find it.

Kitchen Conversions

Quick Basic Conversions

¼ cup = 4 tablespoons
1 tablespoon = 3 teaspoons
½ tablespoon = 1½ teaspoons
Pinch of = ⅟₁₆ teaspoon
1 tablespoon = 15ml
1 teaspoon = 5ml

Measurements

Cup	Tablespoons (tbsp)	Teaspoons (tsp)	Milliliters (ml)
1 cup	16 tbsp	48 tsp	240ml
¾ cup	12 tbsp	36 tsp	180ml
⅔ cup	10 tbsp + 2 tsp	32 tsp	160ml
½ cup	8 tbsp	24 tsp	120ml
⅓ cup	5 tbsp + 1 tsp	16 tsp	80ml
¼ cup	4 tbsp	12 tsp	60ml
–	1 tbsp	3 tsp	15ml
–	½ tbsp	1½ tsp	7.5ml
–	–	1 tsp	5ml

Temperatures

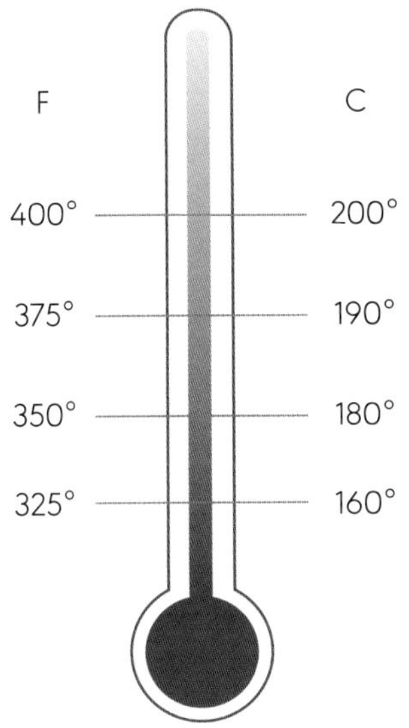

Weights

US Customary (ounces)	1 oz	2 oz	3 oz	4 oz (¼ lb)	5 oz	6 oz	7 oz	8 oz (½ lb)	10 oz	12 oz (¾ lb)	14 oz	15 oz	16 oz (1 lb)
Metric (grams)	28g	55g	85g	115g	140g	170g	200g	225g	285g	340g	395g	425g	455g

Length

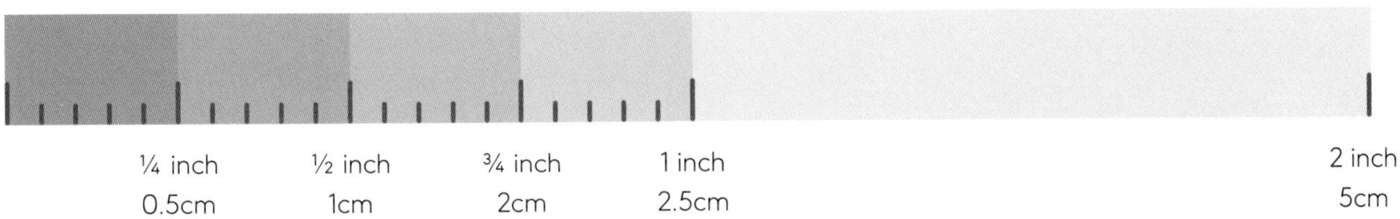

Breakfasts

Energizing Smoothies

Serves 2 — Prep: 5 minutes Cook: 0 minutes Total: 5 minutes

Smoothies are one of my favorite ways to start the day. They're quick, easy, and full of good-for-you nutrition. I tend to use soy milk for the added protein, but any plant milk you enjoy will work just fine. For sweetness, I usually prefer using dates because they sweeten naturally and add fiber. If your blender isn't super strong, you might end up with a few tiny date pieces in your smoothie (which I love!), but if you prefer a completely smooth texture, swap it out for a small splash of maple syrup. For all the smoothie recipes, these are the simple instructions:

1. Place all the ingredients in a blender. Blend until smooth.
2. Pour into glasses and garnish as desired.

Green Energizer Smoothie

1 frozen banana

1½ cups / 225g frozen mango chunks

1 cup / 30g fresh spinach

1 cup / 240ml unsweetened plant milk of choice

¾ cup / 180ml orange juice

1 tablespoon almond butter

Snickers Smoothie

2 frozen bananas

3 Medjool dates, pitted

1½ cups / 360ml unsweetened plant milk of choice

3 tablespoons natural peanut butter

2 tablespoons rolled oats

2 teaspoons cocoa powder, Dutch-process or natural

1 teaspoon pure vanilla extract

Pinch of fine sea salt

Mint Chocolate Chip Smoothie

1½ frozen bananas

½ avocado

1⅓ cups / 40g fresh spinach

2 Medjool dates, pitted

10 fresh mint leaves, plus more to taste

1½ cups / 360ml unsweetened plant milk of choice

1 teaspoon pure vanilla extract

Pinch of fine sea salt

2 tablespoons vegan chocolate chips (see Heads-Up)

HEADS-UP: Start by blending everything except for the chocolate chips, then pulse them in for bits of chocolate in every sip.

Island Life Smoothie

1 frozen banana

1¾ cups / 260g frozen pineapple chunks

¼ cup / 55g seedless frozen passion fruit pulp (see Heads-Up)

1¼ cups / 300ml unsweetened coconut milk beverage

2 tablespoons cashew butter

1 tablespoon hemp seeds

1 teaspoon pure vanilla extract

HEADS-UP: If you're only able to find frozen passion fruit with seeds, first thaw the cubes, strain the seeds, and refreeze.

Toasted Coconut Strawberry Smoothie

2 frozen bananas

1 cup / 150g frozen strawberries

1½ cups / 360ml unsweetened plant milk of choice

3 Medjool dates, pitted

3 tablespoons rolled oats

3 tablespoons unsweetened shredded coconut, toasted

2 tablespoons cashew butter

2 teaspoons pure vanilla extract

Pinch of fine sea salt

High-Protein Peanut Butter & Jelly Smoothie

5.3 ounces / 150g silken tofu

1 frozen banana

1¼ cups / 300ml unsweetened soy or pea milk

1 cup / 130g frozen mixed berries

¼ cup / 65g natural peanut butter

3 tablespoons rolled oats

1½ tablespoons maple syrup

2 teaspoons pure vanilla extract

Snickers Smoothie
Green Energizer Smoothie
Toasted Coconut Strawberry Smoothie

Mint Chocolate Chip Smoothie
Island Life Smoothie
High-Protein Peanut Butter & Jelly Smoothie

Toasted Coconut & Almond Granola

FAN FAVORITE

Makes 6 cups — Prep: 10 minutes Cook: 30 minutes Total: 40 minutes

This granola is an all-time fan favorite on the blog. It was the very first granola recipe I ever shared on the site, and all these years later, it's still the one I make most often. It's become a bit of a weekend ritual in our home: I throw together a batch on Sunday, and breakfast is basically sorted for the rest of the week. I'll add a generous handful to a bowl of yogurt with some fruit, and I'm good to go.

It's endlessly customizable, too. You can swap the almonds for pecans, or stir in different mix-ins after baking, like dried fruit or dark chocolate chips. Once you've got the base down, you can make it your own. Trust me when I say you'll never go back to store-bought granola again.

- 3 cups / 275g rolled oats
- 1 cup / 160g raw almonds, chopped
- ½ cup / 80g raw pumpkin seeds
- ½ cup / 70g raw sunflower seeds
- ¾ cup / 70g unsweetened shredded coconut
- ¼ teaspoon fine sea salt
- ½ cup / 120ml maple syrup
- ¼ cup / 60ml vegetable oil

OPTIONAL ADD-INS
(After Baking)

- Chocolate chips
- Hemp seeds
- Dried cranberries

1. Preheat the oven to 325°F / 160°C. Line a baking sheet with parchment paper.

2. In a large bowl, combine the oats, almonds, pumpkin seeds, sunflower seeds, coconut, and salt. Add the maple syrup and oil, and mix well to coat everything evenly. Spread the mixture onto the prepared baking sheet.

3. Bake for about 30 minutes, or until lightly golden. Stir twice during baking to ensure even toasting.

4. Let cool completely on the baking sheet. The granola will continue to crisp up as it cools. Once cooled, stir in any add-ins you like. If adding chocolate, be sure the granola is completely cool to prevent it from melting.

Gluten-Free Buckwheat Crêpes

Makes 8 crêpes — Prep: 5 minutes Cook: 20 minutes Total: 25 minutes

This isn't your classic crêpe recipe. Traditional batters often need time to rest so the gluten in the flour can relax, but since this one's made with buckwheat flour, which is naturally gluten-free, there's no need to wait. And the impatient part of me loves that about it. The batter comes together in minutes and goes straight from the bowl to the pan. Buckwheat adds a boost of protein, fiber, and nutrients, and gives the crêpes a lovely earthy, nutty flavor. They're especially delicious topped with nut butter, chocolate spread, jam, fresh fruit, or a dollop of yogurt.

1¼ cups / 300ml unsweetened plant milk of choice, plus more as needed

1 cup / 140g buckwheat flour

3 tablespoons sugar

½ teaspoon pure vanilla extract

¼ teaspoon fine sea salt

1 tablespoon unsalted vegan butter, for the pan

OPTIONAL FILLINGS AND TOPPINGS

Nut butter

Chocolate spread

Jam

Fresh fruit

Plant-based yogurt

1. In a large bowl, whisk together the milk, buckwheat flour, sugar, vanilla, and salt until smooth. The batter should have the texture of coconut milk. If it's too thick, add a little more milk, 1 tablespoon at a time, until it pours smoothly from a spoon.

2. Heat a crêpe pan or nonstick medium skillet over medium-high heat and lightly grease with a bit of the butter.

3. Pour about ¼ cup / 60ml of batter into the pan, swirling it to evenly coat the surface in a thin layer. Cook for 2 to 3 minutes, until the underside is golden. Flip the crêpe and cook for 1 to 2 minutes, until the second side is golden as well. Transfer to a plate and cover with a clean kitchen towel to keep warm. Repeat with the remaining batter, adding a bit of the butter to the pan as needed.

4. Fill and top the crêpes as desired.

Spinach Crêpes
with Lemon Pea Whip

Makes 8 crêpes — **Prep:** 15 minutes **Cook:** 30 minutes **Total:** 45 minutes

This recipe was born of a very beige breakfast rut, when nearly everything we were making—toast, oatmeal, granola—was some shade of brown. These vibrant green crêpes get their color from a big handful of spinach, but don't worry, they don't taste "green." Their mild flavor makes them the perfect canvas for your favorite fillings. Go sweet if that's your mood, or enjoy them savory with a creamy lemon whip for a double protein boost from tofu and peas.

SPINACH CRÊPES

2 cups / 60g fresh spinach

1½ cups / 360ml soy or almond milk, plus more as needed

2 teaspoons white vinegar

1 cup / 135g all-purpose flour

1 teaspoon baking powder

¼ teaspoon fine sea salt

Olive oil, for the skillet

SAUTÉED PEAS

1 teaspoon olive oil

1 cup / 140g frozen green peas

½ teaspoon garlic powder

½ teaspoon onion powder

LEMON PEA WHIP

Grated zest and juice of ½ lemon

1 tablespoon olive oil

7 ounces / 200g firm tofu

1 tablespoon nutritional yeast flakes

1 teaspoon maple syrup

1 teaspoon white miso paste

¼ teaspoon fine sea salt

1. **MAKE THE SPINACH CRÊPES:** In a blender, combine the spinach, milk, and vinegar and blend until smooth.

2. In a large bowl, combine the flour, baking powder, and salt. Place a sieve over the bowl and pour in the spinach mixture. (This helps catch any unblended bits and ensures a silky-smooth batter.) Stir until just combined, being careful not to overmix. The batter should have the texture of coconut milk. If it's too thick, add a little more milk, 1 tablespoon at a time, until it pours smoothly from a spoon.

3. In a crêpe pan or nonstick medium skillet, heat a drizzle of olive oil over medium-high heat. Pour in about ⅓ cup / 80ml of the batter, swirling the pan to coat the surface in a thin, even layer. Cook until lightly golden on both sides, 1 to 2 minutes per side. Repeat with the remaining batter, adding a drizzle of oil to the pan in between crêpes as needed.

4. **SAUTÉ THE PEAS:** In a small sauté pan, combine the oil, peas, garlic powder, and onion powder. Cook over medium-high heat, stirring occasionally, for 5 minutes to thaw the peas. Set aside half of the peas and pour the remaining peas into a blender for the lemon pea whip.

5. **MAKE THE LEMON PEA WHIP:** To the peas in the blender, add the lemon zest, lemon juice, oil, tofu, nutritional yeast, maple syrup, miso, and salt. Blend until smooth.

6. Fill the crêpes with the pea whip and serve topped with the reserved peas.

HEADS-UP: If you've got some leftover tofu, the Tofu Vermicelli Noodle Bowls with Peanut Sauce (page 178) is a great way to use it up.

Banana Chocolate Chunk Pancakes

Makes about 12 pancakes — Prep: 10 minutes Cook: 20 minutes Total: 30 minutes

Nothing says weekend like a stack of pancakes, and for me, the best kind always includes chocolate (obviously). But be careful: Don't mix the chocolate into the batter (I learned that the hard way). If the chocolate touches the hot pan, it doesn't melt, it scorches. So here's a little trick: Pour the batter into the pan first, sprinkle the chocolate on top, then add just a little more batter to cover them. That way, the chocolate stays safely tucked inside, away from the heat. No burning, just melty pockets in all the right places. These pancakes are perfect for a cozy weekend morning or a special brunch. Optionally, dress them up with caramelized banana slices on top.

2 bananas
1⅓ cups / 320ml unsweetened soy or pea milk
1 tablespoon apple cider vinegar
2 teaspoons pure vanilla extract
1½ cups / 205g all-purpose flour
2 tablespoons sugar
1 tablespoon baking powder
¼ teaspoon fine sea salt
Vegetable oil, for the pan
1 ounce / 28g dairy-free dark chocolate, chopped
Fresh berries (optional), for serving
Maple syrup (optional), for serving

1. In a medium bowl, mash 1 of the bananas until mostly smooth. Stir in the milk, vinegar, and vanilla until well mixed.

2. In a large bowl, sift together the flour, sugar, baking powder, and salt. Pour the milk mixture into the flour mixture and stir until just combined.

3. Chop half of the remaining banana (reserve the other half). In a crêpe pan or nonstick medium skillet, heat a drizzle of oil over medium-high heat. Scoop about 3 tablespoons of batter onto the pan for each pancake. Top with a few pieces of the chopped banana and chocolate. Spoon about 1 tablespoon of batter over the banana and chocolate pieces to cover them (and prevent them from burning when flipped).

4. Cook for 1 to 2 minutes, until the top is bubbling and the bottom is golden. Then flip and cook on the other side until golden. Repeat with the remaining batter, adding a drizzle of oil to the pan as needed.

5. If desired, serve the pancakes with fresh berries and a drizzle of maple syrup, or your favorite toppings.

6. **OPTIONAL:** You can simply slice the remaining half banana and serve it as a topping. Or if you're feeling extra, caramelize the slices: Heat a small skillet over medium heat with a tiny drizzle of oil or a small pat of vegan butter. Add the banana slices in a single layer and cook until golden and lightly caramelized on both sides, 1 to 2 minutes per side.

HEADS-UP: For the fluffiest results, stick with soy or pea milk here. Both are high in protein, which helps the pancakes hold their lift and keep a light texture. We tested a version with almond milk (low in protein), and while still tasty, the pancakes came out flatter and a bit gummy. So not all plant milks are created equal. Gotta love a little food science in the kitchen!

Creamy Curried "Egg" Salad Bowls

FAN FAVORITE

Serves 2 — Prep: 15 minutes Cook: 10 minutes Total: 25 minutes

For those who prefer savory over sweet in the morning, this one's for you. It's a simplified take on a fan favorite from our blog, built around my husband Robin's soft and fluffy vegan "egg" salad that's received so much love over the years. In this simplified version, I've paired it with a quick and tangy arugula salad that's simple, nourishing, and easy enough to make any day of the week.

½ English cucumber, chopped

1 cup / 150g cherry tomatoes, quartered

1½ tablespoons extra-virgin olive oil

1 tablespoon apple cider vinegar

½ tablespoon maple syrup

Fine sea salt

1 teaspoon vegetable oil

14 ounces / 395g firm tofu, pressed (see How to Press Tofu, page 37)

⅛ teaspoon ground turmeric

⅛ teaspoon freshly ground black pepper, plus more to taste

⅓ cup plus 1 tablespoon / 95g vegan mayonnaise, plus more to taste

¾ teaspoon curry powder

1 green onion, white part minced, green tops sliced

2 cups / 40g arugula

1 avocado, sliced

2 large slices rustic bread, toasted

1. In a medium bowl, combine the cucumber, tomatoes, olive oil, vinegar, maple syrup, and a pinch of salt. Set aside to soak up the flavors.

2. In a large skillet, heat the vegetable oil over medium-high heat. Crumble the tofu into the pan using your hands and cook for 5 to 7 minutes, stirring occasionally, until the tofu is soft and spongy but not too crispy.

3. Sprinkle in ½ teaspoon salt, the turmeric, and pepper and cook for 1 to 2 minutes more, stirring constantly to toast the spices.

4. Remove from the heat and transfer the tofu to a medium bowl. Stir in the mayo and curry powder. Taste and add more salt and mayo if you like. Add the white part of the green onion and stir it into the tofu "egg" salad.

5. Add the arugula to the bowl with the cucumber and tomatoes. Toss to combine.

6. Assemble the bowls with the "egg" salad, arugula salad, sliced avocado, and toast. Garnish with the reserved green onion tops and more salt and pepper to taste.

HEADS-UP: For an extra eggy flavor, sprinkle a bit of kala namak (also called black salt) over the top just before serving. Black salt has a naturally sulfurous taste that gives dishes that classic hard-boiled egg flavor.

Die Freien Demokraten wünschen Gerstenmaiers Rücktritt

Corn & Feta Toasts

with Blistered Tomatoes

Makes 6 toasts — Prep: 15 minutes Cook: 10 minutes Total: 25 minutes

I always forget how much I love canned corn until I crack open a can and use it in something like this. It's nothing fancy, but it tastes like something you'd order at a brunch place. The spread comes together by blending canned sweet corn with tofu and a bit of feta to make a base that's high in protein with just the right amount of texture. Layered on top are cherry tomatoes cooked down with garlic until soft, blistered, and sweet. Don't worry: The garlic loses its sharpness as it cooks so it won't leave you with morning garlic breath. And while the toppings might seem simple, please don't be tempted to treat any of them as optional. Every single one is needed to round out the flavors.

- 5.6 ounces / 160g firm tofu
- 2½ ounces / 70g vegan feta
- 1 tablespoon apple cider vinegar
- ½ tablespoon nutritional yeast flakes
- 1 teaspoon onion powder
- ¼ teaspoon fine sea salt
- 1 (15-ounce / 425g) can corn kernels, drained and rinsed
- 6 slices whole wheat bread
- ½ tablespoon olive oil, plus more (optional) for toasting the bread
- 3 cups / 455g cherry tomatoes
- 2 garlic cloves, crushed to a paste
- ¼ cup / 4g fresh basil, sliced
- ¼ teaspoon chile flakes
- ⅛ teaspoon freshly ground black pepper

1. In a food processor, combine the tofu, feta, vinegar, nutritional yeast, onion powder, and salt. Blend until smooth. Add the corn and pulse a few times, just until incorporated. The goal is to retain some texture, so avoid overblending.

2. Toast the bread as desired. (For added flavor and crispness, try toasting it in a skillet with a small drizzle of olive oil.)

3. In a medium pan, heat the oil over medium-high heat. Add the tomatoes and cook for about 5 minutes, until they start to blister. Add the garlic and cook for 2 minutes more.

4. Spread the corn mixture over the toasted bread. Top with the blistered tomatoes, basil, chile flakes, black pepper, and more salt to taste.

Butter Bean Shakshuka

Serves 2 — Prep: 10 minutes Cook: 20 minutes Total: 30 minutes

Shakshuka is a beloved Middle Eastern dish traditionally made with poached eggs in a rich tomato and bell pepper sauce, seasoned with warm and fragrant spices. In this plant-based version, the eggs are swapped for lima beans (also known as butter beans), which add a creamy texture and a boost of plant-based protein. Assuming you have a few staples in your pantry, the shopping list is blissfully short: one bell pepper, a bit of cilantro, and some bread to scoop it all up. It's hearty, comforting, and best of all, everything comes together in one pan.

1 tablespoon vegetable oil
1 medium onion, finely chopped
2 garlic cloves, minced
1 tablespoon harissa paste
1 tablespoon tomato paste
1 red bell pepper, chopped
1 (14.5-ounce / 410g) can crushed tomatoes
1 (15-ounce / 425g) can lima beans (butter beans), drained and rinsed
1 teaspoon sugar
½ teaspoon fine sea salt
¼ cup / 4g fresh cilantro (optional), chopped
2 large slices rustic bread, toasted, for serving

1. In a sauté pan, heat the oil over medium-high heat. Add the onion and cook for 5 to 7 minutes, until golden.
2. Stir in the garlic, harissa paste, and tomato paste and cook for 2 minutes more, stirring often to prevent sticking.
3. Add the bell pepper, tomatoes, beans, sugar, and salt and simmer for 5 to 8 minutes, until the sauce thickens and the peppers are tender to your liking.
4. Taste and add more salt if you like. Stir in the cilantro (if using) and serve warm with toasted bread.

Creamy Chai Oatmeal

Serves 2 —— Prep: 10 minutes Cook: 15 minutes Total: 25 minutes

Chai has always felt like home to me. I grew up around a lot of Indian culture, and when I was living in Toronto as a kid, there was this Indian market I used to visit with my sister. We'd spend ages choosing which Bollywood movie to rent—picking up boxes, reading the backs, changing our minds more than a few times. Once we finally settled on one, we'd reward ourselves with a chai latte from the little shop next door. It was this cozy blend of steamed milk, black tea, and fragrant spices that warmed us from the inside out and made the perfect end to our outings. With this creamy chai oatmeal, I wanted to bring that same feeling of comfort and nostalgia to the breakfast table. It's like a chai latte you can eat with a spoon.

1¾ cups / 420ml unsweetened plant milk of choice (I use soy)

1 teaspoon loose-leaf black tea in a tea infuser, or 1 black teabag

1 star anise

½ teaspoon ground cinnamon

¼ teaspoon ground ginger

¼ teaspoon ground cardamom

Pinch of fine sea salt

Pinch of freshly ground black pepper

3 tablespoons maple syrup

¾ cup / 60g quick-cooking oats

½ tablespoon unsalted vegan butter

1 pear, cut into ½-inch / 1cm cubes

½ cup / 130g unsweetened coconut yogurt

OPTIONAL TOPPINGS

Unsweetened coconut flakes, toasted

Roasted walnuts

Cacao nibs

1. In a medium saucepan, combine the milk, tea infuser (or teabag), star anise, cinnamon, ginger, cardamom, salt, black pepper, and 2 tablespoons of the maple syrup. Bring to a gentle simmer over medium heat and cook for 3 to 5 minutes, until fragrant. Remove and discard the tea and star anise.

2. Stir in the oats and cook uncovered, stirring frequently to prevent sticking, for about 5 minutes, or until the oats are tender and the mixture is creamy.

3. Meanwhile, in a small skillet, melt the butter over medium heat. Add the pear and cook for 3 to 5 minutes, until softened. Set aside.

4. In a small bowl, combine the yogurt and the remaining 1 tablespoon maple syrup.

5. To serve, spoon the chai-spiced oatmeal into bowls. Top with the sweetened yogurt and warm pears. Add any optional toppings you'd like.

Blended Tiramisu Oats

Serves 1 —— Prep: 10 minutes Cook: 0 minutes Total: 10 minutes

Yes, you can have dessert for breakfast, and yes, it can be nourishing, too. This tiramisu-inspired recipe blends rolled oats with plant milk, espresso, and dates to create a creamy, dreamy base—no cooking required. And while it might seem odd to eat oats without cooking them first, rolled oats are actually steamed during processing, so they're not raw and don't *need* to be cooked again. Topped with a swirl of yogurt and a dusting of cocoa powder, it's everything you love about tiramisu, just in a breakfast-friendly form.

½ cup / 46g rolled oats

3 Medjool dates, pitted

½ cup / 120ml unsweetened plant milk of choice

¼ cup / 60ml brewed espresso or strong pour-over coffee

1 teaspoon ground flaxseeds

2 teaspoons pure vanilla extract

Pinch of fine sea salt

½ cup / 130g unsweetened coconut yogurt

½ tablespoon almond butter

1 teaspoon maple syrup

½ teaspoon Dutch-process or natural cocoa powder

1. In a blender, blend the oats into a coarse flour. Add the dates, milk, espresso, flaxseeds, 1 teaspoon of the vanilla, and salt. Blend until smooth and then pour into a serving bowl.

2. In a small bowl, stir together the yogurt, almond butter, maple syrup, and remaining 1 teaspoon vanilla until well combined.

3. Layer this yogurt mixture over the blended oats. Finish with a dusting of cocoa powder on top. No need to cook or chill, it's ready to enjoy right away!

Handhelds

Baked Chipotle Chickpea Flautas
with Avocado Crema

FAN FAVORITE

Makes 6 flautas — **Prep:** 20 minutes **Cook:** 20 minutes **Total:** 40 minutes

This recipe took off the moment we shared it and quickly became a fan favorite. Inspired by Mexican flautas, this version is a little lighter: baked instead of fried (but still deliciously crisp!) and filled with a spicy and smoky plant-based bean and chipotle mix in place of the usual meat. We've made them for weeknights, game nights, and cozy weekends in—and every time, they disappear fast.

FILLING

1 (15-ounce / 425g) can chickpeas, drained and rinsed

½ cup / 90g canned kidney beans

1 small red onion, finely chopped

Juice of ½ lime

3 tablespoons minced chipotle peppers in adobo sauce

2 tablespoons nutritional yeast flakes

2 tablespoons ketchup

1 tablespoon taco seasoning

¼ teaspoon fine sea salt

ASSEMBLY

6 (8-inch / 20cm) soft flour tortillas

1 tablespoon vegetable oil

AVOCADO CREMA

1 avocado, halved and pitted

1 garlic clove, peeled but whole

¼ cup / 65g unsweetened soy or almond yogurt

Juice of ½ lime

¼ teaspoon fine sea salt

1 cup / 240g pico de gallo, for serving

1. Preheat the oven to 400°F / 200°C. Line a baking sheet with parchment paper.

2. **MAKE THE FILLING:** In a medium bowl, combine the chickpeas, beans, onion, lime juice, chipotles, nutritional yeast, ketchup, taco seasoning, and salt. Mash well with a fork until well mixed, leaving some texture for bite.

3. **ASSEMBLE THE FLAUTAS:** Dividing evenly, spoon a line of the mashed filling along one side of each tortilla. Roll each up tightly, then place seam-side down on the prepared baking sheet. Brush the tops lightly with the oil and transfer to the oven.

4. Bake for 15 to 20 minutes, until golden.

5. **MEANWHILE, MAKE THE AVOCADO CREMA:** Scoop the avocado flesh into a small food processor. Add the garlic, yogurt, lime juice, and salt and blend until smooth. (Alternatively, mash the avocado in a bowl first, then crush the garlic to a paste and mix it into the avocado along with the yogurt, lime juice, and salt.)

6. Serve the baked flautas with the pico de gallo and avocado crema.

HEADS-UP: If you've got leftover chipotles in adobo, put them to good use in the Spicy Pulled Mushroom Tacos (page 69).

Spicy Pulled Mushroom Tacos
with Jalapeño Lime Aioli

Makes 9 tacos — Prep: 25 minutes Cook: 15 minutes Total: 40 minutes

Oyster mushrooms cook down into a surprisingly meaty texture that works beautifully as taco filling. The trick is to let them hang out in the pan a little longer than you think, until the chipotle coating starts to brown. Finish with dollops of creamy jalapeño mayo to balance the heat, and you've got a new Taco Tuesday favorite.

PULLED MUSHROOMS

1 pound / 455g oyster mushrooms

1 tablespoon vegetable oil

1 garlic clove, crushed to a paste

3 tablespoons minced chipotle peppers in adobo sauce

SALSA

2 medium tomatoes, chopped

1 garlic clove, minced

Juice of ¼ lime

2 tablespoons fresh cilantro leaves, chopped

⅛ teaspoon fine sea salt

JALAPEÑO LIME AIOLI

⅓ cup / 80g vegan mayonnaise

½ jalapeño, seeded

Juice of ¼ lime

1 garlic clove, peeled but whole

ASSEMBLY

9 (6-inch / 15cm) soft flour tortillas, warmed

1 cup / 240g refried beans

2 heads Little Gem lettuce or 1 romaine heart, chopped

½ cup / 100g pickled red onions

1. **PREPARE THE PULLED MUSHROOMS:** Tear the oyster mushrooms into strips and add them to a medium sauté pan over medium-high heat. Dry-sauté for 8 to 10 minutes, until the mushrooms are soft and any released liquid has evaporated.

2. Stir the oil, garlic, and chipotles into the mushrooms. (The tacos pack a bit of heat, so consider adding less chipotle if a milder heat is preferred.) Cook for 4 to 5 minutes more, until golden.

3. **MAKE THE SALSA:** In a medium bowl, combine the tomatoes, garlic, lime juice, cilantro, and salt and mix well.

4. **MAKE THE JALAPEÑO LIME AIOLI:** In a small food processor, combine the mayo, jalapeño, lime juice, and garlic and blend until smooth.

5. **ASSEMBLE THE TACOS:** Layer each tortilla with a spread of refried beans, followed by lettuce, salsa, mushrooms, pickled onions, and a few dollops of jalapeño lime aioli.

Eggplant Caponata & Hummus Wraps

Makes 5 wraps — **Prep:** 10 minutes **Cook:** 25 minutes **Total:** 35 minutes

I love traveling through Mediterranean countries, but finding vegan food isn't always the easiest. One day, while I was in Sicily, I came across caponata, which is a sweet-and-sour vegetable dish with eggplant as the star ingredient. I ordered it at a little café, and it was love at first bite. It was one of those dishes that makes you pause between bites just to appreciate what's going on.

While it's traditionally served as an antipasto, we adapted it by loading it into a wrap and adding hummus to make a complete meal. The hummus isn't a traditional pairing, but I love the creamy texture and extra plant-based protein it brings. This one's easy to prep, and the filling holds up well in the fridge, so you can make it in advance and build your wraps when hunger strikes.

- ½ tablespoon olive oil
- 1 medium onion, thinly sliced
- 1 small eggplant, cut into 1-inch / 2.5cm pieces
- 2 jarred roasted red peppers, chopped (see Heads-Up)
- 1 (14.5-ounce / 410g) can whole peeled tomatoes
- ⅓ cup / 45g pitted kalamata olives, chopped
- ¼ cup / 40g raisins
- 2 tablespoons capers
- ½ teaspoon fine sea salt
- 1 cup / 245g hummus
- 5 (10-inch / 25cm) soft flour tortillas, warmed
- 2 tablespoons roasted pine nuts
- 2 tablespoons fresh basil leaves, coarsely torn

1. In a large sauté pan, heat the oil over medium-high heat. Stir in the onion and cook for 5 minutes, until lightly golden.

2. Stir in the eggplant, roasted peppers, tomatoes, olives, raisins, capers, and salt. Cook for about 15 minutes, until the eggplant is tender and the sauce has thickened.

3. Spread some hummus on the warmed wraps, then load up with caponata and finish with some pine nuts and basil.

HEADS-UP: Our jarred roasted red peppers are packed in a vinegar brine, which gives the caponata its signature tang. If your jarred roasted peppers are oil-packed or not very tangy, consider adding a small splash of red wine vinegar to taste.

Chickpea Waldorf Wraps

Makes 2 wraps — Prep: 15 minutes Cook: 0 minutes Total: 15 minutes

I know fruit in savory recipes can be divisive, but there's something I really love about the way its sweetness and juiciness add contrast, and this wrap delivers that twofold with both apples and grapes. It's loosely inspired by the classic Waldorf salad, but with a creamy chickpea and hummus filling added to make it heartier and more balanced as a full meal. I usually prefer using red apples for their extra bit of natural sweetness, but any variety you enjoy will do. Perfect for lunch, a picnic, or a quick bite on the go.

½ cup / 80g cooked chickpeas
½ cup / 125g hummus
¼ cup / 38g red grapes, halved
½ red apple, finely chopped
1 celery rib, finely chopped
2 tablespoons roasted walnuts, chopped
2 tablespoons vegan mayonnaise
¼ teaspoon celery salt
Pinch of freshly ground black pepper
6 butter lettuce leaves
2 (10-inch / 25cm) soft flour tortillas, warmed

1. In a large bowl, mix together the chickpeas, hummus, grapes, apple, celery, walnuts, mayo, celery salt, and pepper.

2. Divide the lettuce between the warmed tortillas, then spoon the filling on top. Fold in the sides, then roll the tortilla tightly to close.

Sticky Loaded Tempeh Flatbread

Serves 4 — Prep: 15 minutes Cook: 15 minutes Total: 30 minutes

Meet tempeh at its best: sticky, saucy, spicy, and surrounded by crunchy, creamy, and tangy ingredients to perfectly complement it. If you've ever been unsure about tempeh, I get it. If it's not prepared well, it can taste a bit dry or earthy. The first few times I cooked it, I wasn't exactly sold. But two things changed that. First: Give it plenty of sauce. Tempeh really shines when it has something flavorful clinging to it. Second: Tear it into rough chunks instead of slicing it neatly. The jagged edges catch more sauce, and with the help of the maple syrup, it all caramelizes in the pan into something full of depth and flavor.

TEMPEH

2 (8-ounce / 225g) packages tempeh

3 tablespoons vegetable oil

¼ teaspoon fine sea salt

¼ cup / 60ml ketchup

2 tablespoons maple syrup

2 tablespoons soy sauce

2 tablespoons sriracha

1 tablespoon rice vinegar

2 teaspoons cornstarch

AVOCADO CREAM

2 avocados, halved and pitted

¼ cup / 65g unsweetened soy or almond yogurt

¼ cup / 4g fresh cilantro

1 garlic clove, peeled but whole

½ tablespoon rice vinegar

⅛ teaspoon fine sea salt

ASSEMBLY

4 medium flatbreads, toasted

⅓ cup / 65g pickled red onions

⅓ cup / 49g unsalted roasted peanuts, chopped

Fresh cilantro (optional), for garnish

1. **COOK THE TEMPEH:** Tear the tempeh roughly into 1-inch / 2.5cm chunks.

2. In a large sauté pan, dry-sauté the tempeh over medium-high heat to warm it. Add the oil and salt and cook the tempeh for 7 to 8 minutes, until golden.

3. Meanwhile, in a small bowl, mix together the ketchup, maple syrup, soy sauce, sriracha, vinegar, and cornstarch until smooth.

4. Once the tempeh is golden, add the sauce and cook, stirring to coat, for 2 to 3 minutes more, until the sauce thickens and turns sticky.

5. **MAKE THE AVOCADO CREAM:** Scoop the avocado flesh into a small food processor. Add the yogurt, cilantro, garlic, vinegar, and salt and blend until smooth.

6. **ASSEMBLE THE FLATBREADS:** Spread the avocado cream onto the flatbreads, then top with the sticky tempeh, pickled red onions, chopped peanuts, and cilantro (if using).

Vegan "Tuna" Sandwiches

FAN FAVORITE

Makes 2 sandwiches — Prep: 20 minutes Cook: 0 minutes Total: 20 minutes

This lunchbox classic, made the plant-based way, has become a fan favorite in our app. Re-creating the unique flavor of tuna isn't easy, but this version comes very close, and in some ways, dare I say, even improves on the original. One reader commented, "As a vegan I'm usually skeptical of fish alternatives, but this was SUPERB. I'd be fooled in a blind taste test."

It combines mashed chickpeas with creamy mayo, crunchy celery, and finely chopped nori to mimic the familiar taste of the sea. If you're not a huge fan of seaweed, start with half the amount. You can always add more to taste later. And if your knife isn't up to the task, try snipping the seaweed with scissors or pulsing it in a spice grinder. But whatever you do: Don't skip the pickles!

- 1 (15-ounce / 425g) can chickpeas, drained and rinsed
- 1 celery rib, finely chopped
- 1 nori seaweed sheet, finely chopped
- ¼ small red onion, finely chopped
- ¼ cup / 60g vegan mayonnaise
- ¼ cup / 36g chopped pickles
- 2 teaspoons reduced-sodium soy sauce
- 1 teaspoon rice vinegar
- ½ teaspoon garlic powder
- ¼ teaspoon fine sea salt
- 4 butter lettuce leaves
- 4 slices whole wheat bread, toasted
- 2 small radishes (optional), thinly sliced

1. In a medium bowl, mash the chickpeas with a fork until mostly broken down, leaving some texture. Mix in the celery, seaweed, onion, mayo, pickles, soy sauce, vinegar, garlic powder, and salt. Taste and add more salt if you like.

2. Place 2 lettuce leaves on each of 2 slices of toasted bread. Spoon a generous amount of the "tuna" mixture on top, add sliced radishes (if using), and close the sandwiches with the remaining pieces of toast.

Smashed Green Peas & Mint Toasts

Makes 4 toasts — Prep: 10 minutes Cook: 5 minutes Total: 15 minutes

I'm quite literally obsessed with this toast, and while peas on toast might sound a little odd, trust me when I say the mix of creamy, tangy, salty, and herby flavors is unexpectedly addictive. For the best result, I suggest using frozen peas instead of canned as they keep the color vibrant and the taste fresh. Toasting the bread in a pan with a splash of oil makes the bread extra tasty, though the toaster works just fine if you're short on time. When I'm serving it to guests, I like to finish with a few extra mint leaves and thinly sliced radish to make it feel a little more special. It's the perfect fresh light meal or snack.

2 cups / 275g frozen green peas
1 tablespoon olive oil
4 slices multigrain bread
Juice of ½ lemon
¼ cup / 4g fresh parsley leaves, finely chopped
2½ ounces / 70g vegan feta, crumbled (about ½ cup)
2 tablespoons unsweetened soy or almond yogurt
1 tablespoon vegan green pesto (see Heads-Up)
1 tablespoon fresh mint leaves, finely chopped
1 teaspoon Dijon mustard
¼ teaspoon garlic powder
¼ teaspoon chile flakes, plus more (optional) for garnish
¼ teaspoon fine sea salt
Pinch of freshly ground black pepper
4 small radishes (optional), thinly sliced

1. Place the peas in a heatproof medium bowl and pour plenty of boiling water over them. Set aside to thaw for about 10 minutes.

2. In a large skillet, heat the oil over medium-high heat. Toast the bread slices for about 2 minutes per side, or until golden on both sides.

3. Drain the peas and transfer them to a medium bowl. Mash them with a fork until mostly broken down, leaving a bit of texture. Stir in the lemon juice, parsley, feta, yogurt, pesto, mint, mustard, garlic powder, chile flakes, salt, and black pepper.

4. Spoon a generous amount of the pea mixture onto the toasted bread. If desired, top with radishes and a few extra chile flakes for added heat.

HEADS-UP: We used a store-bought pesto to keep things quick, but if you'd rather make it yourself at home, I recommend our Basil Cashew Pesto (page 134).

Curry-Stuffed Pita Pockets

Makes 6 stuffed pitas — Prep: 10 minutes Cook: 20 minutes Total: 30 minutes

This one-pan recipe takes all the comfort of a creamy curry and tucks it into a soft, warm pita pocket. It's definitely not the most traditional way to enjoy curry, but it makes for a fun, filling, and easy handheld meal. Of course, it's just as tasty on its own with rice or naan if that's more your style. Just a heads-up, it can get a bit messy, and to keep the bread from becoming soggy, wait to stuff the pitas until just before serving. It's great for meal prep, too. Just store the curry in the fridge and warm it up when you're ready to feast.

½ tablespoon vegetable oil
1 medium onion, finely chopped
2 garlic cloves, crushed to a paste
3 tablespoons tomato paste
1 teaspoon sweet paprika
1 teaspoon ground cumin
½ teaspoon ground coriander
¼ teaspoon chile flakes
1 red bell pepper, chopped
1 (15-ounce / 425g) can brown lentils, drained and rinsed
1 vegetable bouillon cube, crumbled
1 cup / 240ml canned full-fat coconut milk
3 cups / 90g fresh baby spinach
6 (4-inch / 10 cm) pita breads, warmed
¼ cup / 4g fresh parsley (optional), chopped
¼ cup / 30g shredded vegan mozzarella cheese (optional)

1. In a large sauté pan, heat the oil over medium-high heat. Add the onion and cook for 4 minutes, or until lightly golden.

2. Add the garlic and tomato paste and cook for 2 minutes more, stirring frequently, until the paste darkens slightly. Add the paprika, cumin, coriander, and chile flakes and cook, stirring, for another minute to toast the spices. Add the bell pepper, lentils, bouillon, and coconut milk. Simmer uncovered for 8 to 10 minutes to thicken.

3. Stir in the spinach and cook until wilted.

4. Slice open part of the warmed pita bread to create little pockets. Fill with the lentil mixture. If desired, top with parsley and vegan mozzarella.

Green Summer Rolls
with Peanut Sauce

Makes 9 rolls — Prep: 40 minutes Cook: 5 minutes Total: 45 minutes

Every summer, I crave anything and everything that's crisp and refreshing, and these green salad rolls are a recipe I make on repeat. They're as fresh as fresh can get. They're also great for sharing and entertaining. The first time I served them, I thought I'd made way too much peanut sauce . . . until everyone started dunking their rolls so generously that it disappeared in no time. It's so good, you'll want to drink it.

PEANUT SAUCE

Juice of 1 lime

½ cup / 130g natural peanut butter

½ cup / 120ml water

2 tablespoons reduced-sodium soy sauce

1½ tablespoons sriracha

1 teaspoon maple syrup

ROLLS

2 teaspoons toasted sesame oil

6 ounces / 170g broccolini, cut into 3-inch / 7.5cm pieces

2 garlic cloves, crushed to a paste

⅛ teaspoon fine sea salt

9 rice paper sheets

¾ English cucumber, julienned

2 ounces / 55g butter lettuce leaves, roughly torn into large pieces (about 2 cups)

1½ cups / 135g fresh bean sprouts

⅓ cup / 5g fresh mint leaves, stems removed

⅓ cup / 5g fresh cilantro leaves, stems removed

1. **MAKE THE PEANUT SAUCE:** In a small bowl, whisk together the lime juice, peanut butter, water, soy sauce, sriracha, and maple syrup. It will start very loose, but will thicken the more you stir it.

2. **PREPARE THE ROLLS:** In a medium sauté pan, heat the sesame oil over medium-high heat. Add the broccolini, garlic, and salt and cook for 4 to 5 minutes, until the broccolini is tender.

3. Fill a large bowl with lukewarm water. Submerge one sheet of rice paper for 3 to 4 seconds. It will continue to soften when taken out of the water (see Heads-Up).

4. Place the rice paper sheet on a plate. Layer some sautéed broccolini, cucumber, lettuce, bean sprouts, mint, and cilantro in the center. Fold in the sides, then roll it up tightly from the bottom. Cut in half with a sharp knife.

5. Repeat with remaining ingredients. Serve with the peanut dipping sauce on the side.

HEADS-UP: When working with rice paper, use lukewarm water (not hot!) and dip each sheet for just a few seconds. If it sits too long, it can turn overly soft, sticky, and fragile, making it harder to roll without tearing. It should still feel slightly firm when taken out of the water. As you pile on the filling, it'll continue to soften to the right texture. If the first roll isn't picture-perfect, don't be discouraged. I always see it as a practice roll anyway. Once you've done one, the rest come together more easily.

Mango Tofu Lettuce Wraps

Makes 8 lettuce wraps — **Prep:** 20 minutes **Cook:** 15 minutes **Total:** 35 minutes

This recipe was created by one of the recipe developers in our test kitchen. The first time we made it, we laid everything out family-style and sat around the table to dig in. Within minutes, the platter was wiped clean. The tofu was sticky, sweet, and saucy—no surprise, since the original version had ¼ cup of brown sugar. It was undeniably good, but when revisiting it for the cookbook, we wondered if we could bring a bit more balance without sacrificing flavor.

So, we played around. We halved the sugar and added mango for a fresh burst of natural sweetness. The wraps are still just as sweet and saucy, but now more of that sweetness comes from whole fruit. Honestly, playing with these kinds of tweaks is one of my favorite parts of recipe development.

2 garlic cloves, crushed to a paste

¼ cup / 60ml reduced-sodium soy sauce

3 tablespoons water

2 tablespoons light brown sugar

1 tablespoon rice vinegar

2 teaspoons cornstarch

1 teaspoon grated fresh ginger

1 tablespoon vegetable oil

14 ounces / 395g firm tofu, pressed (see How to Press Tofu, page 37)

3 ounces / 85g rice vermicelli noodles

8 butter lettuce leaves

½ carrot, peeled into ribbons

1 cup / 90g shredded red cabbage

½ mango, thinly sliced into ribbons

OPTIONAL GARNISHES

Toasted sesame seeds

Sliced green onion

Fresh cilantro

1. In a small bowl, mix together the garlic, soy sauce, water, sugar, vinegar, cornstarch, and ginger.

2. In large skillet, heat the oil over high heat. Crumble in the tofu and cook for about 8 minutes, or until golden. Pour in the sauce and cook, stirring constantly, for about 2 minutes, or until thickened and the tofu is well coated.

3. Place the rice noodles in a large heatproof bowl and cover with boiling water. Let soak for 2 to 3 minutes, until tender. Drain the noodles and rinse under cold water to stop the cooking process.

4. To assemble, layer a lettuce leaf with rice noodles, saucy tofu, fresh veggies, and mango ribbons. Garnish as desired.

HEADS-UP: This is a super-flexible recipe! Swap in rice for noodles, cucumber for carrot, or toss in some edamame for extra protein.

Lemongrass Seitan Bánh Mì

Makes 3 sandwiches — Prep: 20 minutes Cook: 10 minutes Total: 30 minutes

There was a popular bánh mì sandwich shop under my sister's apartment in Canada, and I'd always swing by to grab a couple of subs before heading up to visit her. Now an ocean away from that shop, I make my own twist on the Vietnamese classic when the craving strikes. Instead of the usual meat filling, this recipe uses the plant-based protein powerhouse: seitan, in a sweet lemongrass marinade. The pickled veggies, or đồ chua, add an essential crunch and tang, so don't skip them.

PICKLED VEGGIES

- ½ **carrot,** julienned
- **2½ ounces / 70g daikon radish,** julienned (see Heads-Up)
- **½ cup / 120ml white vinegar**
- **½ cup / 120ml boiling water**
- **1 tablespoon light brown sugar**

MARINATED SEITAN

- **1 stalk lemongrass**
- **Juice of 1 lime**
- **1 small shallot,** quartered
- **2 garlic cloves,** peeled but whole
- **3 tablespoons reduced-sodium soy sauce**
- **2 tablespoons light brown sugar**
- **2 tablespoons vegetable oil**
- **1 tablespoon chopped fresh ginger**
- **7 ounces / 200g seitan,** torn into chunks

ASSEMBLY

- **3 tablespoons vegan mayonnaise**
- **1 tablespoon sriracha**
- **3 sandwich buns,** such as kaiser rolls or small baguettes, toasted
- **¼ English cucumber,** sliced
- **Crispy fried shallots (optional),** for garnish

1. **MAKE THE PICKLED VEGGIES:** In a jar, combine the carrot, daikon, vinegar, boiling water, and sugar. Set aside for 20 minutes to pickle.

2. **MARINATE THE SEITAN:** Trim the fibrous end of the lemongrass and remove the tough outer layers. In a small food processor, blend the lemongrass, lime juice, shallot, garlic, soy sauce, brown sugar, oil, and ginger.

3. Place the seitan in a medium bowl and pour the marinade over the top. Stir and let sit for at least 10 minutes.

4. Heat a large nonstick pan over medium-high heat. Add the seitan along with the marinade and cook, stirring occasionally, for 7 to 8 minutes, until the sauce is sticky and the seitan is lightly caramelized.

5. **ASSEMBLE THE SANDWICHES:** In a small bowl, mix together the mayo and sriracha. Spread onto both sides of the toasted buns. Layer with cucumber slices, seitan, pickled veggies, and fried shallots (if using).

HEADS-UP: If you can't find daikon, small red radishes or cucumbers work, too; or just double up on the carrot. For the bread, I used kaiser rolls in the photo, but traditional Vietnamese baguettes work just as well.

Sun-Dried Tomato Tofu Turnovers

Makes 8 turnovers — Prep: 30 minutes Cook: 20 minutes Total: 50 minutes

We sometimes run little challenges in our test kitchen to keep things fun and push our creativity. One day, the task was to come up with a five-ingredient recipe (not counting the basics like salt and pepper). Not an easy limit to stick to! The winning five: tofu, garlic, spinach, sun-dried tomatoes, and puff pastry. We wrapped them up, baked them off, and dunked them into a homemade tzatziki. The tray was polished off in minutes.

When re-creating the recipe for this cookbook, we loosened the rules a bit. A handful of olives went in (because let's be honest, I'll find any excuse to add olives), along with some oregano to lean into Mediterranean flavors, *aaaand* a sprinkle of sesame seeds on top just to make them look a touch fancy. They're easy to pick up and eat, perfect for parties, game nights, or whenever you're craving a savory, golden, flaky snack.

- 14 ounces / 395g firm tofu, pressed (see How to Press Tofu, page 37)
- 4 garlic cloves, crushed to a paste
- ½ cup / 55g frozen spinach, thawed, drained, and squeezed dry
- ¼ cup / 38g oil-packed sun-dried tomatoes, drained and finely chopped
- 4 tablespoons oil from the sun-dried tomato jar (or supplement with olive oil)
- ¼ cup / 34g pitted kalamata olives, finely chopped
- ½ tablespoon dried oregano
- ¾ teaspoon fine sea salt
- ¼ teaspoon freshly ground black pepper
- 1 pound / 455g vegan puff pastry dough, thawed if frozen
- 1 tablespoon sesame seeds

1. Place the tofu in a large bowl and mash with the back of a fork until crumbly. Stir in the garlic, spinach, sun-dried tomatoes, 2 tablespoons of the sun-dried tomato oil, the olives, oregano, salt, and pepper.

2. Preheat the oven to 400°F / 200°C. Line two baking sheets with parchment paper.

3. Cut the puff pastry into eight 5-inch / 12cm squares. Arrange the squares on the lined baking sheets.

4. Divide the tofu mixture evenly among the squares, spooning it into the center of each one. Fold each pastry into a triangle and press the edges closed with a fork. Brush the tops with the remaining 2 tablespoons sun-dried tomato oil (or olive oil) and sprinkle with the sesame seeds. Transfer to the oven.

5. Bake until golden, 20 to 25 minutes, flipping the turnovers and swapping the sheets between racks halfway through.

6. Let the turnovers cool slightly before serving.

"Chicken" Parm Panini

Makes 3 panini — Prep: 20 minutes Cook: 35 minutes Total: 55 minutes

Back when I worked at an Italian American pasta restaurant, eating chicken parm over spaghetti was my end-of-shift ritual. It was my comfort food. This recipe is a plant-based spin on that nostalgic meal, turned into a cozy panino. Instead of the usual breaded chicken, I use tofu, baked until golden and crisp, then layer it with classic marinara, melted vegan cheese, and serve it on warm toasted ciabatta. You could also easily serve it over pasta instead.

BREADED TOFU

14 ounces / 395g firm tofu, pressed (see How to Press Tofu, page 37)

⅓ cup / 43g cornstarch

2 teaspoons dried oregano

1 teaspoon garlic powder

¼ teaspoon fine sea salt

¼ teaspoon freshly ground black pepper

½ cup / 120ml unsweetened soy or almond milk

⅔ cup / 38g panko bread crumbs

Cooking spray

MARINARA SAUCE

1 cup / 240g canned crushed tomatoes

2 tablespoons fresh basil, chopped

½ tablespoon garlic powder

½ tablespoon sugar (optional)

¼ teaspoon fine sea salt

ASSEMBLY

6 vegan cheese slices (we used mozzarella-style cheese)

3 small ciabattas, split and toasted

⅔ cup / 20g fresh baby spinach

1. Preheat the oven to 425°F / 220°C. Line a baking sheet with parchment paper.

2. **MAKE THE BREADED TOFU:** Slice the tofu lengthwise into 6 pieces, each about ½ inch / 1cm thick.

3. Set up a breading station in three shallow bowls: In the first bowl, mix the cornstarch, oregano, garlic powder, salt, and pepper. Pour the milk into a second bowl. Scatter the panko in the third.

4. Coat each tofu slice first in the cornstarch mixture, then dip into the milk, and finally press into the panko to coat. Place the breaded tofu on the prepared baking sheet. Lightly spritz each slab with cooking spray and transfer to the oven.

5. Bake until golden, 25 to 30 minutes, flipping halfway through.

6. **MEANWHILE, MAKE THE MARINARA SAUCE:** In a small saucepan, combine the crushed tomatoes, basil, garlic powder, sugar (if using), and salt. Bring to a gentle simmer over medium-low heat and cook, uncovered, for about 15 minutes, or until slightly thickened.

7. **ASSEMBLE THE PANINI:** Once the tofu is golden, top each piece with a slice of cheese and return to the oven for about 5 minutes, or until melted.

8. On the bottom half of each split ciabatta, layer some spinach, followed by the breaded tofu. Spoon the warm marinara sauce over the top and close the sandwich with the other side of the ciabatta.

Salads

Roasted Beet & Feta Salad

Serves 4 — Prep: 15 minutes Cook: 1 hour 30 minutes Total: 1 hour 45 minutes

I have a bit of an obsession with beets now, but funny enough, they were my least favorite veg growing up. I still remember the first time they won me over. It was a casual get-together with friends, and someone showed up with a roasted beet salad. The roasting mellowed out that earthy flavor and brought out a natural sweetness I didn't know beets could have. I've been hooked ever since. This recipe is my take on that dish, with the addition of creamy feta for a salty contrast. The best part is, it's mostly hands-off. Let the oven do all the heavy lifting so that you can get ready to fall in love with beets, just as I did.

1¾ pounds / 800g beets (about 4 medium beets)

½ tablespoon vegetable oil

Juice of 1 lemon

2 garlic cloves, crushed to a paste

3 tablespoons extra-virgin olive oil

½ tablespoon maple syrup

1 teaspoon Dijon mustard

¼ teaspoon fine sea salt

⅛ teaspoon freshly ground black pepper

1 ounce / 28g vegan feta, crumbled (about ¼ cup), plus more for garnish

Fresh parsley (optional), for garnish

1. Preheat the oven to 400°F / 200°C.

2. Peel the beets and cut them into ½-inch / 1cm cubes. Place in a baking dish, coat with the vegetable oil, and cover with a lid or foil. Transfer to the oven.

3. Roast for 1 hour 20 minutes to 1 hour 30 minutes, until fork-tender. Let cool.

4. Meanwhile, in a small bowl, mix together the lemon juice, garlic, olive oil, maple syrup, mustard, salt, and pepper.

5. Transfer the roasted beets to a large bowl and pour in the dressing. Crumble the feta over the top and toss to coat.

6. If desired, serve garnished with more feta and parsley.

Zucchini Ribbon Salad

with Pesto Cream

Serves 4 — Prep: 25 minutes Cook: 15 minutes Total: 40 minutes

This salad looks like something you'd order at a restaurant, but it's surprisingly simple to make. Perfect for spring or summer, it combines juicy cherry tomatoes (I like a mix of cherry tomatoes in shades of red, orange, and yellow), delicate zucchini ribbons, and crunchy croutons, all layered on a bed of creamy cashew pesto. It's great as a side, but honestly, hearty enough to enjoy as a meal on its own.

⅔ cup / 85g raw cashews

SALAD

2 tablespoons extra-virgin olive oil

Grated zest and juice of 1 lemon

2 garlic cloves, crushed to a paste

¼ teaspoon fine sea salt

1 medium zucchini

1 (15-ounce / 425g) can cannellini beans, drained and rinsed

1 yellow bell pepper, chopped

2⅔ cups / 400g cherry tomatoes, halved

CRUNCHY CROUTONS

4 large slices rustic bread, cut into cubes

2 tablespoons vegetable oil

¼ teaspoon fine sea salt

Pinch of freshly ground black pepper

PESTO CREAM

¾ cup / 180ml unsweetened soy or almond milk

½ cup / 120g vegan green pesto

⅛ teaspoon fine sea salt

Fresh basil (optional), for garnish

1. Cover the cashews with plenty of boiling water and set them aside to soften while you prepare the other salad components.

2. Preheat the oven to 350°F / 180°C.

3. **PREPARE THE SALAD:** In a large bowl, combine the olive oil, lemon zest, lemon juice, garlic, and salt.

4. Use a vegetable peeler to cut the zucchini lengthwise into thin ribbony strips, then cut the long ribbons in half crosswise. Add the zucchini ribbons to the bowl of dressing along with the beans, bell pepper, and tomatoes. Toss and let marinate while you bake the croutons.

5. **BAKE THE CRUNCHY CROUTONS:** Line a baking sheet with parchment paper. Add the bread cubes, vegetable oil, salt, and pepper and toss to coat. Bake until golden, about 15 minutes, flipping halfway.

6. **MAKE THE PESTO CREAM:** Drain the cashews and transfer them to a blender and add the milk, pesto, and salt. Blend until smooth. Taste and add more salt if you like.

7. To serve, spoon the pesto cream into the bottom of each serving bowl, then layer the marinated veggie/bean mixture on top. Add the croutons and garnish with some fresh basil (if using).

Roasted Potato Salad
with Caramelized Onion Dressing

Serves 6 — Prep: 15 minutes Cook: 45 minutes Total: 1 hour

One of my biggest love languages is sharing food. I'm never one to get possessive over what's on my plate. If something I'm eating catches your eye, I'm more than happy to share. But this salad might be the exception. It's so good that giving any up, even just a little, feels like a real test of my generosity. The dressing might well be the best part. It starts with a pan of slow-caramelized onions, then gets hit with a splash of rice vinegar, soy sauce, and maple syrup—a little tangy, a little savory, a little sweet. Once it simmers down and thickens slightly, it gets tossed with crisp, fresh veggies to balance the warm, golden roasted potatoes. My love for caramelized onions is only matched by my love for potatoes, and bringing the two together is pure heaven.

- 2 pounds 2 ounces / 1kg baby potatoes, quartered
- 3 tablespoons vegetable oil
- ¼ teaspoon fine sea salt
- 1 large onion (10½ ounces / 300g), thinly sliced
- ⅓ cup / 80ml rice vinegar
- 2 tablespoons reduced-sodium soy sauce
- 2 tablespoons maple syrup
- 1 tablespoon toasted sesame seeds
- ¼ teaspoon chile flakes
- 2 cups / 40g arugula
- ½ cup / 8g fresh cilantro, finely chopped
- 8 small radishes, thinly sliced
- 2 green onions, thinly sliced
- ½ English cucumber, chopped

1. Preheat the oven to 400°F / 200°C. Line a baking sheet with parchment paper.

2. Place the potatoes on the lined sheet. Drizzle with 1 tablespoon of the oil, sprinkle with the salt, and toss to coat.

3. Roast for 40 to 45 minutes, until the potatoes are golden. Let cool slightly before adding to the salad.

4. Meanwhile, in a large sauté pan, heat the remaining 2 tablespoons oil over medium-high heat. Add the onion and cook, stirring occasionally, for about 15 minutes, or until golden.

5. Reduce the heat to medium-low and stir in the vinegar, soy sauce, maple syrup, sesame seeds, and chile flakes. Simmer for 6 to 8 minutes, until the sauce thickens. Set aside to cool slightly.

6. In a large bowl, combine the arugula, cilantro, radishes, green onions, cucumber, roasted potatoes, and caramelized onion dressing. Toss to combine before serving.

Mediterranean Pasta Salad

Serves 4 to 6 — Prep: 10 minutes Cook: 15 minutes Total: 25 minutes

Everyone needs to have a good, simple pasta salad recipe. It's the kind of dish that feels right at home at picnics, potlucks, or packed into lunchboxes. One of our testers told us her husband loved this recipe so much, he was eating it straight out of the mixing bowl before she could even plate it. What a seal of approval!

Fine sea salt

3 cups / 225g fusilli pasta

DRESSING

¼ cup / 60ml extra-virgin olive oil

3 tablespoons red wine vinegar

2 garlic cloves, minced

1 tablespoon capers, chopped

½ teaspoon dried oregano

½ teaspoon flaky sea salt

¼ teaspoon freshly ground black pepper

SALAD

1 (15-ounce / 425g) can black-eyed peas, drained and rinsed

½ cup / 70g pitted kalamata olives, chopped

½ English cucumber, seeded and sliced

½ small red onion, thinly sliced

⅓ cup / 50g oil-packed sun-dried tomatoes in oil, drained and chopped

¼ cup / 4g fresh dill, minced

1. Bring a large pot of generously salted water to a boil. Add the pasta and cook for 2 to 3 minutes longer than the package recommends for al dente (see Heads-Up).

2. **MEANWHILE, MAKE THE DRESSING:** In a small bowl, stir together the oil, vinegar, garlic, capers, oregano, flaky salt, and pepper. Set aside.

3. Drain and rinse the pasta under cold water to stop the cooking process. Drain well.

4. **ASSEMBLE THE SALAD:** In a large bowl, combine the drained pasta, black-eyed peas, olives, cucumber, red onion, sun-dried tomatoes, and dill. Add the dressing and toss to coat.

5. Serve at room temperature or chilled.

HEADS-UP: Over the years, I've learned a little trick to make pasta salads even better: slightly overcook the pasta by a couple of minutes. As it cools, pasta naturally firms up, and this helps it stay tender instead of turning chewy or stiff. It also helps avoid that chalky, starchy coating you sometimes get when pasta sits.

Summer Barley Salad with Cashew Cream

Serves 4 — Prep: 20 minutes Cook: 30 minutes Total: 50 minutes

I'm a big fan of hearty salads that hold their own as a meal, and this one is my go-to for late summer into early fall. The veggies are lightly cooked, not raw, so the salad feels warm and comforting (though also delicious cold!). It's got chewy barley, hearty lentils, rich cashew cream, and a zingy dressing to tie it all together. And it travels well, too, so it's perfect for packed lunches or weekend picnics.

CASHEW CREAM

¾ cup / 100g raw cashews

1 garlic clove, peeled but whole

¼ cup / 60ml water

1½ tablespoons nutritional yeast flakes

½ tablespoon apple cider vinegar

¼ teaspoon fine sea salt

BARLEY

Fine sea salt

1 cup / 200g pearled barley

DRESSING

3 tablespoons extra-virgin olive oil

2 tablespoons balsamic vinegar

½ tablespoon agave or maple syrup

¾ teaspoon fine sea salt

Pinch of freshly ground black pepper

SALAD

1 tablespoon vegetable oil

1 garlic clove, crushed to a paste

1 yellow bell pepper, chopped

1½ cups / 225g cherry tomatoes, halved

1 medium zucchini, sliced into ¼-inch / 5mm coins

1 (15-ounce / 425g) can brown lentils, drained and rinsed

¼ cup / 4g fresh basil leaves, torn

1. **MAKE THE CASHEW CREAM:** Soak the cashews in plenty of boiling water for 10 minutes to soften. Drain and transfer to a blender.

2. Add the garlic, water, nutritional yeast, vinegar, and salt and blend until smooth. Set aside.

3. **COOK THE BARLEY:** Bring a large pot of generously salted water to a boil. Add the barley, reduce the heat to a gentle simmer, and cook, stirring occasionally, for about 20 minutes, or until the barley is pleasantly chewy and tender. Continue cooking the barley for an extra 2 minutes for a softer texture. Drain and transfer to a large bowl.

4. **MEANWHILE, MAKE THE DRESSING:** In a small bowl, stir together the olive oil, vinegar, agave, salt, and pepper. Set aside.

5. **PREPARE THE SALAD:** In a large skillet, heat ½ tablespoon of the vegetable oil over medium-high heat. Add the garlic, bell pepper, and tomatoes and cook for 5 to 7 minutes, until the tomatoes start to burst. Transfer to the large bowl with the barley.

6. Add the remaining ½ tablespoon vegetable oil to the now-empty pan. Working in batches, cook the zucchini in a single layer until golden on both sides, 5 to 8 minutes per side. Transfer to the large bowl.

7. Add the lentils to the large bowl and toss to combine.

8. To serve, sprinkle the basil over the salad, add dollops of the cashew cream, and pour the dressing over the top. Mix well and serve.

Roasted Sweet Potato & Kale Salad

FAN FAVORITE

Serves 4 — Prep: 15 minutes Cook: 30 minutes Total: 45 minutes

When we first shared this recipe, it immediately went viral. Maybe because of its proven ability to turn kale skeptics into kale fans. One of the comments we got was, "Best salad I've had in ages! I never really liked raw kale, but I decided to try it one more time, and I'm so very glad I did. I believe you have converted me!" That about sums it up.

ROASTED SWEET POTATO

3 medium sweet potatoes (1 pound 5 ounces / 600g total), cut into ½-inch / 1cm cubes

1 medium red onion, sliced

4 garlic cloves, unpeeled

1 teaspoon vegetable oil

1 teaspoon ground cumin

½ teaspoon sweet paprika

¼ teaspoon fine sea salt

Pinch of ground black pepper

DRESSING

Juice of 1 lemon

6 fresh mint leaves, thinly sliced

1 tablespoon extra-virgin olive oil

1 tablespoon apple cider vinegar

1 tablespoon maple syrup

½ teaspoon onion powder

¼ teaspoon fine sea salt

KALE SALAD BASE

1 tablespoon extra-virgin olive oil

1 large bunch curly kale, stemmed, leaves chopped (about 4 cups)

1 (15-ounce / 425g) can chickpeas, drained and rinsed

1 avocado, diced

¼ cup / 35g unsalted roasted almonds, chopped

1. **ROAST THE SWEET POTATOES:** Preheat the oven to 425°F / 220°C. Line a baking sheet with parchment paper.

2. Place the sweet potato cubes, red onion, garlic, vegetable oil, cumin, paprika, salt, and pepper on the sheet and toss to coat.

3. Bake until the potatoes are tender, about 30 minutes, stirring halfway through. When the garlic is cool enough to handle, peel them and save for the dressing. Let the sweet potatoes cool slightly.

4. **MAKE THE DRESSING:** In a medium bowl, combine the lemon juice, mint, olive oil, vinegar, maple syrup, onion powder, and salt. Mash the roasted garlic cloves and mix them into the dressing.

5. **PREPARE THE KALE SALAD BASE:** In a large bowl, drizzle the olive oil over the kale and massage the leaves with your hands for 1 to 2 minutes, until softened (see Heads-Up).

6. Add the sweet potatoes to the bowl along with the chickpeas, avocado, and dressing. Toss everything to combine.

7. Top with the roasted almonds and serve.

HEADS-UP: Massaging the kale breaks down its toughness and reduces bitterness. Just 1 minute with a drizzle of olive oil does the trick.

Peanut Crunch Salad

Serves 4 —— Prep: 30 minutes Cook: 0 minutes Total: 30 minutes

In my mid-twenties, I spent half a year backpacking through Southeast Asia—starting in Thailand and ending in Indonesia—and the food from that trip still lives rent-free in my memory. In Thailand, I fell in love with the fruity, spicy, crunchy salads piled high with herbs. In Indonesia, I discovered gado-gado, a warm vegetable salad served with the most savory, peanutty sauce. This salad isn't traditional to either country, but it's a fusion of the parts I loved most: crisp veg, juicy mango, fresh herbs, and a creamy peanut dressing. It's something I could happily eat on repeat.

PEANUT DRESSING

¼ cup / 65g natural peanut butter

1 garlic clove, crushed to a paste

Juice of ½ lime

2 tablespoons water

1½ tablespoons reduced-sodium soy sauce

½ tablespoon sriracha

½ tablespoon agave or maple syrup

SALAD BASE

2 cups / 180g shredded green cabbage

2 green onions, thinly sliced

1 mango, julienned

1 large carrot, julienned

⅔ English cucumber, julienned

½ cup / 8g fresh cilantro, chopped

FOR SERVING

1 cup / 55g crispy fried onions

⅓ cup / 49g salted roasted peanuts, chopped

1. **MAKE THE PEANUT DRESSING:** In a small bowl, mix together the peanut butter, garlic, lime juice, water, soy sauce, sriracha, and agave.

2. **PREPARE THE SALAD BASE:** In a large bowl, combine the green cabbage, green onions, mango, carrot, cucumber, and cilantro.

3. **TO SERVE:** Drizzle the peanut sauce over the salad and toss to coat. Top with the crispy fried onions and chopped peanuts.

Curried Potato Salad

Serves 4 to 6 — Prep: 20 minutes Cook: 15 minutes Total: 35 minutes

One of the most common questions we get is, "What do you do with all that food?" I think of it as our responsibility to share it—with our team, our studio neighbors, and our friends—because every person brings valuable feedback. Nothing ever goes to waste. One Friday evening, after a full day of testing, some friends came by and I set out samples of every dish we'd made. This salad—a creamy mix of potatoes, warm curry spices, crisp veg, and just a hint of sweetness from apple—was the one that got the biggest reaction. When only a small scoop was left, one friend claimed it: "If no one's called dibs, that's mine." Seconds later, another friend helped himself to a spoonful, and the mock outrage that followed had everyone laughing. Safe to say, this salad has earned its place in the rotation. The best part is that the flavors only get better with time, making this a perfect dish to prep ahead.

2 pounds 3 ounces / 1kg baby potatoes, quartered

Fine sea salt

1 tablespoon olive oil

2 garlic cloves, crushed to a paste

1½ tablespoons curry powder

Juice of ½ lemon

½ cup / 120g vegan mayonnaise

2 tablespoons unsweetened soy or almond milk

Pinch of freshly ground black pepper

2 celery ribs, finely chopped

1 yellow bell pepper, chopped

1 red or green apple, finely chopped (see Heads-Up)

¼ cup / 4g fresh parsley, finely chopped

OPTIONAL GARNISHES

Chile flakes

Fresh parsley

1. Place the potatoes in a large pot of salted water. Bring to a gentle boil and cook for about 15 minutes, or until tender. Drain and set aside.

2. Meanwhile, in a small pan, heat the oil over medium-high heat. Add the garlic and sauté for 2 minutes, until fragrant. Add the curry powder and cook for 1 more minute, stirring constantly to toast evenly.

3. Transfer the spiced garlic mixture to a small bowl and whisk in the lemon juice, mayo, milk, ½ teaspoon salt, and black pepper. Set aside.

4. In a large bowl, combine the drained potatoes, celery, bell pepper, apple, and parsley. Pour the dressing over the salad and toss to coat.

5. If desired, garnish with chile flakes and more chopped parsley and serve.

HEADS-UP: We tested this salad with both red and green apples, and it was nearly a 50/50 split on which was preferred—though green had a slight edge for its tartness. That said, if you'd prefer a sweeter contrast to the warm spices, go with red.

Fennel Blueberry Salad

Serves 4 —— Prep: 15 minutes Cook: 0 minutes Total: 15 minutes

Side salads are often an afterthought: a handful of greens, a few tomatoes, and done. But they can be so much more. This one gives fennel the attention it deserves, with its crisp texture and delicate, licorice-like sweetness. Blueberries make a double appearance here: Some stay whole in the salad, while others are blended into the dressing for a subtle, fruity lift. Just be sure to blend the blueberries right before serving, because the natural pectins will cause the dressing to thicken if it sits too long. As the fennel soaks up the deep purple hues, it transforms into something surprisingly beautiful. It's a bit sweet, a little peppery, and full of crunch.

SALAD

1 medium fennel bulb (about 8 ounces / 225g), thinly sliced

3 cups / 60g arugula

1 cup / 150g blueberries

¼ cup / 31g roasted walnuts, roughly chopped

BLUEBERRY DRESSING

Juice of ½ lemon

½ cup / 75g blueberries

1½ tablespoons extra-virgin olive oil

½ tablespoon balsamic vinegar

½ tablespoon agave

¼ teaspoon fine sea salt

Pinch of freshly ground black pepper

1. **PREPARE THE SALAD:** In a large bowl, combine the sliced fennel, arugula, blueberries, and walnuts.

2. **WHEN READY TO SERVE, MAKE THE BLUEBERRY DRESSING:** In a small food processor, blend the lemon juice, blueberries, olive oil, vinegar, agave, salt, and pepper until smooth. Immediately pour the dressing over the salad and toss to coat.

Vegan Caesar Salad

FAN FAVORITE

Serves 4 — **Prep:** 20 minutes **Cook:** 0 minutes **Total:** 20 minutes

Call me basic, but Caesar salad will always be one of my favorite salads. It's a classic for a reason: crisp romaine, a creamy, garlicky dressing, and plenty of crunch. This version is a quicker take on the one that's already popular on our website. That recipe calls for charring the romaine, but here we're keeping it simple by chopping the lettuce instead. Same big flavor, even less effort. Throw it together as a side, or add your favorite protein and call it dinner.

DRESSING

½ cup / 65g raw cashews, soaked overnight (see Heads-Up)

⅓ cup / 80ml water

Grated zest and juice of 1 lemon

3 garlic cloves, peeled but whole

2½ tablespoons nutritional yeast flakes

1 tablespoon extra-virgin olive oil

1 tablespoon apple cider vinegar

2 teaspoons capers

1 teaspoon Dijon mustard

1 teaspoon reduced-sodium soy sauce

⅛ teaspoon freshly ground black pepper

VEGAN PARMESAN

¼ cup / 33g raw cashews

2 teaspoons nutritional yeast flakes

⅛ teaspoon onion powder

⅛ teaspoon fine sea salt

SALAD

4 heads Little Gem lettuce or 2 romaine hearts, chopped

1 cup / 50g croutons, store-bought or homemade (see Lemony Asparagus Soup, page 119)

1. **MAKE THE DRESSING:** Drain the cashews and transfer to a blender. Add the water, lemon zest, lemon juice, garlic, nutritional yeast, olive oil, vinegar, capers, mustard, soy sauce, and pepper and blend until smooth.

2. **MAKE THE VEGAN PARMESAN:** In a small food processor, pulse the cashews, nutritional yeast, onion powder, and salt until finely crumbled.

3. **ASSEMBLE THE SALAD:** Place the chopped lettuce in a large bowl. Drizzle with the dressing and toss to coat. Sprinkle with the vegan parmesan and croutons and serve.

HEADS-UP: The dressing blends best if you soak the cashews the night before. But honestly, if I forget, I just cover them in plenty of boiling water and let them soak for as long as I can, even if it's just 10 minutes. The sauce might not be quite as smooth, but it still tastes ah-mazing.

Soups

Spicy Corn & Coconut Soup

Serves 4 — Prep: 5 minutes Cook: 25 minutes Total: 30 minutes

Corn doesn't get nearly enough love. Growing up, I only ever ate it on the cob in summer, slathered with lime juice, salt, and hot sauce. Beyond that, it rarely made it onto my plate. But lately, I've been more and more drawn to it. Maybe it's the nostalgia of summer days, or maybe it's how effortlessly it adds natural sweetness to a dish. And with frozen, canned, or fresh kernels, it's easy to enjoy year-round—use whatever's most convenient.

2 teaspoons vegetable oil

1 medium onion, chopped

6 garlic cloves, thinly sliced

2 teaspoons ground cumin

1 teaspoon chile powder, or less for less spicy (see Heads-Up)

1 teaspoon sweet paprika

½ teaspoon ground coriander

7 cups / 1.1kg corn kernels, fresh, frozen, or canned

4 cups / 960ml vegetable broth

1 cup / 240ml canned full-fat coconut milk

Juice of 2 limes

¼ teaspoon fine sea salt

OPTIONAL GARNISHES

Fresh cilantro

Tortilla chips

Sliced fresh jalapeño

1. In a large pot, heat the oil over medium-high heat. Add the onion and garlic and cook, stirring, for 3 to 4 minutes, until the onion becomes translucent.

2. Add the cumin, chile powder, paprika, and coriander and cook, stirring constantly, until fragrant, about 1 minute. Add the corn and cook, stirring occasionally, for about 5 minutes, or until lightly browned. Remove the pot from the heat.

3. Transfer half of the corn mixture to a blender along with the vegetable broth. Blend until smooth. (Alternatively, use an immersion blender to blend half of the soup in the pot.) Pour the blended soup back into the pot. Return the pot to a simmer over medium heat and cook another 5 minutes, or until slightly thickened.

4. Stir in the coconut milk, lime juice, and salt. Taste and add more salt if you like. Cook just to heat through.

5. Ladle into bowls and garnish with any or all of the toppings.

HEADS-UP: As the title suggests, I like this soup spicy—and this recipe uses chile powder, spelled with an "e." That's the pure, ground chile pepper kind, not to be confused with chili powder (with an "i"), which is a milder spice blend that usually includes cumin, paprika, garlic, and oregano. For this soup, go with the pure, spicy kind.

Lemony Asparagus Soup

Serves 4 —— Prep: 20 minutes Cook: 30 minutes Total: 50 minutes

As winter fades and the first signs of spring appear, I start craving foods that are both cozy and refreshing. This soup delivers on both—packed with bright, vibrant flavors, all swirled with the natural creaminess of cashews that make the base so comforting. For the perfect finishing touch, I love serving it with quick and crunchy pan-fried croutons for a satisfying contrast in textures.

SOUP BASE

½ tablespoon olive oil

1 medium onion, chopped

4 garlic cloves, minced

1½ pounds / 700g asparagus, trimmed and cut into ½-inch / 1cm pieces (see Heads-Up)

4 cups / 960ml vegetable broth

1 cup / 130g raw cashews

CRUNCHY CROUTONS

2 tablespoons olive oil

2 large slices (150g total) rustic bread, cut into ½-inch / 1cm pieces

1 teaspoon garlic powder

¼ teaspoon sweet paprika

¼ teaspoon fine sea salt

TO FINISH

Juice of 1 lemon

1½ cups / 24g fresh basil leaves

¼ teaspoon freshly ground black pepper

OPTIONAL GARNISHES

Lemon zest

Fresh basil

Extra-virgin olive oil

1. **MAKE THE SOUP BASE:** In a large pot, heat the oil over medium-high heat. Add the onion and garlic and cook for 3 to 4 minutes, until the onion is translucent.

2. Add the asparagus and cook for 5 minutes, until it turns bright green and just starts to soften.

3. Add the vegetable broth and cashews and bring to a boil. Reduce the heat to medium-low, cover, and simmer gently for 15 to 20 minutes, until the asparagus is easily pierced with a fork.

4. **MEANWHILE, MAKE THE CROUTONS:** In a large skillet, heat the oil over medium-high heat. Add the bread, garlic powder, paprika, and salt and cook for 4 to 6 minutes, until the bread is crispy. Set aside.

5. **TO FINISH:** Add the lemon juice, basil, and pepper to the soup. Use an immersion blender or countertop blender to blend until smooth.

6. Ladle the soup into bowls and top with the croutons. Serve with any or all of the garnishes.

HEADS-UP: If desired, you can reserve some of the asparagus tips for garnish. Simply fry them in a touch of oil until golden.

Curried Chickpea Butternut Soup

FAN FAVORITE

Serves 4 — Prep: 20 minutes Cook: 30 minutes Total: 50 minutes

I love meals that taste even better the next day—which is saying something, considering how good this one is straight off the stove. This soup is rich and warmly spiced, with tender butternut squash, fresh tomatoes, and pantry staples like canned chickpeas and coconut milk. It's cozy and satisfying, and I find myself coming back to it all the time. While you could serve it as a side, I almost always enjoy it as a full meal with garlic naan on the side to soak up every last bite.

SPICE MIXTURE

1 tablespoon curry powder

2 teaspoons garam masala

1 teaspoon ground coriander

1 teaspoon ground cumin

½ teaspoon ground turmeric

¼ teaspoon chile flakes

SOUP

1 small butternut squash (1½ pounds / 680g)

1 tablespoon vegetable oil

1 medium onion, chopped

3 garlic cloves, minced

2 teaspoons grated fresh ginger

1½ pounds / 680g tomatoes (about 6 medium), chopped

2 cups / 480ml vegetable broth

½ teaspoon fine sea salt

2 cups / 330g cooked or canned chickpeas

1 (13.5-ounce / 400ml) can full-fat coconut milk

FOR SERVING (optional)

Fresh cilantro

Fresh lemon juice

Vegan Garlic Naan (page 174)

1. **MAKE THE SPICE MIXTURE:** In a small bowl, combine the curry powder, garam masala, coriander, cumin, turmeric, and chile flakes. Having them ready will help prevent burning when added later. Set aside.

2. **MAKE THE SOUP:** Peel and seed the squash and cut into ½-inch / 1cm cubes (about 3¾ cups).

3. In a large pot, heat the oil over medium-high heat. Add the onion and garlic and cook for 3 to 4 minutes, until the onion is translucent.

4. Add the ginger and the spice mixture and cook, stirring constantly, for 1 to 2 minutes to toast the spices. Add the squash, tomatoes, vegetable broth, and salt. Reduce the heat to medium, cover the pot, and simmer for 10 to 12 minutes, until the squash is tender.

5. Use an immersion blender or countertop blender to partially blend the soup. Stir in the chickpeas and coconut milk. Let the soup heat through. Taste and add more salt if you like.

6. Serve as is, or garnish with cilantro and/or a squeeze of fresh lemon juice with some vegan naan on the side.

Tomato & Sweet Potato Gochujang Soup

Serves 4 —— Prep: 10 minutes Cook: 30 minutes Total: 40 minutes

It's always disappointing when you order soup at a restaurant and it falls flat—bland, uninspired, forgettable. In my opinion, soup has endless potential. It can be the highlight of a meal, the dish that steals the show. This one is exactly that—the kind of soup that makes guests pause, raise their eyebrows, and go in for another spoonful. It's bold, spicy, subtly sweet, and packed with umami. Anything but boring.

1 tablespoon vegetable oil

2 medium shallots, chopped

3 garlic cloves, minced

1½ tablespoons gochujang

3 medium sweet potatoes (about 1 lb 5 oz / 600g total), peeled and chopped (about 4 cups)

5 cups / 750g cherry tomatoes, halved

2 cups / 480ml vegetable broth

1 tablespoon reduced-sodium soy sauce

2 teaspoons rice vinegar

2 teaspoons light brown sugar

½ cup / 120ml canned full-fat coconut milk

OPTIONAL GARNISHES

Toasted sesame seeds

Chili crisp

Sliced green onions

1. In a large pot, heat the oil over medium-high heat. Add the shallots and garlic and cook for about 4 minutes, or until lightly golden.

2. Add the gochujang and cook until fragrant, 1 more minute. Add the sweet potatoes, tomatoes, vegetable broth, soy sauce, vinegar, and brown sugar. Cover and bring to a boil. Reduce the heat to medium-low and simmer gently for 15 minutes, or until the sweet potatoes are soft.

3. Use an immersion blender or countertop blender to blend everything until smooth. Add the coconut milk and let the soup heat through over medium heat.

4. Ladle into soup bowls and serve with any or all of the garnishes.

Spinach Mushroom Lasagna Soup

Serves 4 to 6 — Prep: 15 minutes Cook: 20 minutes Total: 35 minutes

I love a good lasagna, but I don't always have 2 hours to spare for layering sauces, fillings, and pasta. On nights when I want all the cozy flavors of lasagna with minimal effort, I turn to lasagna soup. It's hearty enough to be a main, with all the elements of a balanced meal. Mushrooms add a rich, meaty bite, while lima beans—blended into the broth—offer a sneaky yet satisfying boost of protein. Just break in the lasagna sheets and let them soak up the flavorful broth for a bowl of pure comfort.

1 tablespoon olive oil
1 large onion, chopped
6 garlic cloves, minced
1½ tablespoons Italian seasoning
¼ teaspoon chile flakes
3½ cups / 840ml vegetable broth
1 cup / 240ml unsweetened soy or almond milk
1 cup / 170g cooked lima beans (butter beans)
1½ tablespoons white miso paste
6 ounces / 170g cremini mushrooms, sliced (2 cups)
7 ounces / 200g dried lasagna sheets (about 10 sheets)
3 cups / 90g fresh baby spinach
¼ cup / 38g oil-packed sun-dried tomatoes, drained and chopped
2 tablespoons nutritional yeast flakes
⅛ teaspoon freshly ground black pepper
Fine sea salt
Fresh basil (optional), for garnish
Vegan parmesan (optional), for garnish

1. In a large pot, heat the oil over medium-high heat. Add the onion and cook for about 5 minutes, or until lightly golden.

2. Add the garlic, Italian seasoning, and chile flakes and cook for about 2 minutes, until fragrant. Add the vegetable broth, milk, lima beans, and miso paste. Use an immersion blender or countertop blender to blend until smooth (see Heads-Up).

3. Add the mushrooms, then break the lasagna noodles into bite-size pieces directly over the pot as you drop them in. Partially cover and cook, stirring occasionally to prevent the noodles from sticking, for 8 to 10 minutes, until the noodles are al dente.

4. Stir in the spinach, sun-dried tomatoes, nutritional yeast, and black pepper. Cook until the spinach wilts. Season the soup with salt to taste.

5. Ladle the soup into bowls. If desired, garnish with basil and vegan parmesan.

HEADS-UP: The creaminess of the broth depends on how well the lima beans are blended. A high-powered blender works best to get it super smooth. If you're using a less powerful blender, just blend a little longer to help break everything down.

ENTE AI MONUMENTI

Thai Red Curry Coconut Carrot Soup

Serves 4 — Prep: 10 minutes Cook: 25 minutes Total: 35 minutes

Red curry paste is one of the hardest-working ingredients in our pantry. Just a spoonful or two can completely transform a dish; and in this soup, it adds a warm, spicy kick to the sweet and humble carrot base. The ingredient list is almost shockingly simple for how flavorful the end result is. My husband licked the bowl clean when he finished his, and that speaks volumes!

1 tablespoon vegetable oil

1 medium onion, chopped

½ teaspoon fine sea salt

2 garlic cloves, crushed to a paste

1½ tablespoons Thai red curry paste (see Heads-Up)

6 carrots (1¼ pounds/ 650g total), chopped (5 cups)

2½ cups / 600ml vegetable broth

1 (13.5-ounce / 400ml) can full-fat coconut milk

OPTIONAL GARNISHES

Fresh cilantro

Unsalted roasted peanuts

Chile oil

1. In a large pot, heat the oil over medium-high heat. Add the onion and salt and cook for 4 to 5 minutes, until golden. Add splashes of water as needed to deglaze the pot.
2. Add the garlic and curry paste and cook for 2 to 3 minutes, until fragrant.
3. Add the carrots and broth and bring to a boil. Reduce the heat to medium-low, cover, and gently simmer for about 15 minutes, or until the carrots are soft.
4. Add the coconut milk and allow it to heat through. Use an immersion blender or countertop blender to blend the soup until smooth. Taste and add more salt if you like.
5. Ladle the soup into bowls and top with any or all of the garnishes.

HEADS-UP: The heat level in curry paste can vary by brand. If you're sensitive to spice, start with less and add more to taste as you go.

Adasi
(Persian Lentil Soup)

Serves 4 — Prep: 15 minutes Cook: 45 minutes Total: 1 hour, plus 2 hours soaking time

Adasi is a simple, nourishing Iranian lentil soup my mom learned from her mother, and she still makes it the way she always has: by feel. When I first tried to capture the recipe, I stood beside the pot with a notebook, asking "How much?" each time she added an ingredient. She'd laugh and say, "I never measure. You just taste and see what it needs." Eventually, I convinced her to measure it with me so I could write it down. This is the measured version of her unmeasured method, and I'm so glad I recorded it. I make it often whenever I need a taste of home.

1 cup / 205g dry green lentils, rinsed
2 tablespoons vegetable oil
1 large onion, chopped
2 garlic cloves, crushed to a paste
2 tablespoons tomato paste
½ tablespoon ground cumin
1 teaspoon ground turmeric
½ teaspoon ground cinnamon (optional)
½ teaspoon fine sea salt
¼ teaspoon freshly ground black pepper
1 small Yukon Gold potato (optional), peeled and cut into ½-inch / 1cm cubes
4 cups / 960ml vegetable broth, plus more as needed
½ lemon or lime, cut into wedges, for serving

1. Place the lentils in a large bowl and cover with plenty of water. Let them soak on the counter for 2 hours. Drain.

2. In a large pot, heat the oil over medium heat. Add the onion and cook for about 15 minutes, or until golden and caramelized.

3. Add the garlic, tomato paste, cumin, turmeric, cinnamon (if using), salt, and pepper. Cook for 2 minutes, stirring constantly, until the spices are nicely toasted.

4. Add the drained lentils, potato (if using), and vegetable broth and bring to a boil. Reduce the heat to medium-low, cover, and gently simmer for about 30 minutes, or until the lentils are cooked.

5. Optionally, use an immersion blender to blend some of the lentils into a puree, leaving some texture. (Alternatively, transfer about half of the lentils to a countertop blender and puree until smooth, then return it to the pot.)

6. Taste test and adjust the seasoning or liquid as desired. For a thinner adasi, simply add more broth or water. For thicker, simmer uncovered for a few minutes longer.

7. Serve it with a squeeze of lemon or lime juice, and top it with caramelized onions if desired (see Heads-Up).

HEADS-UP: To make the optional caramelized onion topping, sauté 1 medium onion (thinly sliced) in 2 tablespoons of oil with a pinch of salt over medium-low heat for 25 to 30 minutes, stirring often, until deeply golden.

Shiitake Dumpling Soup

Serves 4 —— Prep: 1 hour Cook: 20 minutes Total: 1 hour 20 minutes

As a kid, my husband, Robin, would visit a Chinese restaurant with his dad on special occasions. One of his fondest memories was sharing wonton soup together, and the dumplings were always his favorite part. Inspired by that memory, we developed this soup. It has a rich umami flavor, and while making dumplings might seem intimidating, they're much easier to make than you'd think and surprisingly relaxing once you get into the rhythm.

DUMPLINGS

2 teaspoons vegetable oil

2 green onions, sliced

2 garlic cloves, crushed to a paste

5.3 ounces / 150g firm tofu

2.6 ounces / 75g fresh shiitake mushrooms, minced (1 cup)

1 head baby bok choy, finely chopped (1½ cups)

½ cup / 55g grated carrot (from 1 medium carrot)

½ tablespoon grated fresh ginger

1 tablespoon soy sauce

20 vegan dumpling wrappers

MUSHROOM BROTH

6 cups / 1.4L vegetable broth

1½-inch / 4cm piece fresh ginger, sliced (14g)

1 tablespoon soy sauce, plus more to taste

4 ounces / 115g fresh shiitake mushrooms, sliced (1½ cups)

2 teaspoons toasted sesame oil

ASSEMBLY

4 heads baby bok choy, halved lengthwise

Toasted sesame seeds (optional)

Chili crisp (optional)

1. **MAKE THE DUMPLINGS:** In a large skillet, heat the oil over medium heat. Add the green onions and garlic and cook, stirring constantly, for 2 to 3 minutes, until fragrant and just beginning to turn golden.

2. Crumble the tofu into the pan and add the shiitakes, bok choy, carrot, ginger, and soy sauce. Cook for 3 to 4 minutes, until the veggies are soft. Remove the pan from the heat and let it cool off a little bit.

3. Set a baking sheet or large plate near your work surface. Add about 1 tablespoon of the cooked veggie filling to the middle of each dumpling wrapper. Use a little water to wet the edges and fold the wrapper in half. Press out any extra air before firmly pinching the edges to seal. Bring the two corners of the dumpling together and use a little water to stick them together. Transfer to the baking sheet or plate and cover with a damp kitchen towel while you make the remaining dumplings.

4. **MAKE THE MUSHROOM BROTH:** In a large pot, combine the vegetable broth, ginger slices, soy sauce, and shiitakes and bring to a boil. Reduce the heat to medium-low, cover, and simmer gently for 10 minutes to infuse flavor into the broth. Stir in the sesame oil at the end.

5. **TO ASSEMBLE:** Meanwhile, fill a second large pot with water and bring to a boil. Working in batches to avoid overcrowding, submerge a few of the dumplings and cook until they start to float to the top, which takes about 1 minute. Be careful not to overcook them. Use a slotted ladle to transfer the dumplings to serving bowls. Continue until all the dumplings are cooked. Keep the pot of water at a boil.

6. To the pot of boiling water, add the bok choy for 1 to 2 minutes to blanch. Then remove with a slotted spoon and transfer to the serving bowls.

7. Remove the ginger slices from the broth, then pour the broth into the serving bowls. If desired, garnish with sesame seeds and chili crisp.

Bites & Dips

Fresh Pestos

Makes about 1 cup — Prep: 5 minutes Cook: 0 minutes Total: 5 minutes

These pestos are incredibly versatile—toss them with warm pasta or cold pasta salads, spread them onto sandwiches and wraps, or simply enjoy them as a delicious dip for crackers and crudités! For all the pesto recipes, these are the simple instructions:

1. In a food processor, combine all the ingredients except for the olive oil and blend until finely chopped.
2. With the processor running, stream in the olive oil until the pesto reaches your desired consistency. Avoid over-blending, as this can cause the olive oil to turn bitter.
3. Plate and garnish as desired.

Basil Cashew Pesto

3 cups / 48g fresh basil leaves

½ cup / 70g unsalted roasted cashews

¼ cup / 34g toasted pine nuts

2 garlic cloves, peeled but whole

Juice of ½ lemon

2 tablespoons nutritional yeast flakes

1 teaspoon fine sea salt

½ cup / 120ml extra-virgin olive oil

Red Pepper Olive Pesto

3 jarred roasted red peppers
½ cup / 60g roasted walnuts
¼ cup / 34g kalamata olives, pitted
¼ cup / 38g oil-packed sun-dried tomatoes, drained
1 garlic clove, peeled but whole
Juice of ½ lemon
1 tablespoon nutritional yeast flakes
½ tablespoon red wine vinegar
¾ teaspoon fine sea salt
¼ teaspoon sweet paprika
3 tablespoons extra-virgin olive oil

Mint Pesto

2 cups / 32g fresh mint leaves (about 1 bunch)
1⅔ cups / 27g fresh basil leaves (about 1 bunch)
½ cup / 70g toasted pine nuts
3 garlic cloves, peeled but whole
Juice of ½ lemon
2 tablespoons water
½ tablespoon nutritional yeast flakes
½ teaspoon fine sea salt
¼ cup / 60ml extra-virgin olive oil

Zesty Basil Hemp Pesto

1½ cups / 24g fresh basil leaves
½ cup / 80g hemp seeds
2 garlic cloves, peeled but whole
1 jarred roasted red pepper
Juice of ½ lemon
1 tablespoon nutritional yeast flakes
¼ teaspoon fine sea salt
¼ cup / 60ml extra-virgin olive oil

Lemon Artichoke Pesto

1 cup / 175g marinated artichoke hearts
½ cup / 8g fresh parsley leaves
⅓ cup / 46g unsalted roasted almonds
1 garlic clove, peeled but whole
2 tablespoons nutritional yeast flakes
2 tablespoons water
2 teaspoons fresh lemon juice
½ teaspoon fine sea salt
⅛ teaspoon freshly ground black pepper
⅓ cup / 80ml extra-virgin olive oil

Red Pepper Olive Pesto
Lemon Artichoke Pesto
Mint Pesto

Zesty Basil Hemp Pesto
Basil Cashew Pesto

Garlic Basil Focaccia Muffins

Makes 12 muffins

Prep: 20 minutes **Cook:** 20 minutes
Total: 40 minutes, plus 14 hours resting time

While traditional focaccia is made in a large pan, this version is baked in a muffin pan, which gives each one individual golden crusts and a perfectly portioned shape that makes it easy to transport, snack on, or share. The process is simple and mostly hands-off: The dough rests overnight in the fridge, with a couple of hours of rise time on baking day. As they bake, your kitchen fills with the aroma of garlic, basil, and freshly baked bread. They're soft and chewy on the inside, crisp on the edges, and perfect for picnics, lunchboxes, or a savory snack. A taste of the sunny Mediterranean, right from your own oven.

2 cups / 270g bread flour
1 teaspoon active dry yeast
1 teaspoon fine sea salt
1 cup / 240ml lukewarm water
3 garlic cloves, crushed to a paste
¾ cup / 12g fresh basil leaves, chopped
⅓ cup / 50g plus 3 tablespoons oil-packed sun-dried tomatoes, drained and chopped
Olive oil, as needed
Pinch of flaky sea salt, for garnish

1. In a large bowl, combine the flour, yeast, and fine sea salt. Pour in the water and mix with a rubber spatula until a sticky dough forms. Fold in the garlic, basil, and ⅓ cup / 50g of the sun-dried tomatoes.

2. Lightly rub the dough's surface with some olive oil, cover with a clean, damp kitchen towel, and refrigerate for at least 12 hours, or up to 18 hours.

3. When ready to bake, generously grease 12 cups of a standard muffin tin with oil.

4. Lightly oil your hands and divide the dough among the muffin cups. Brush the tops with a bit more oil to prevent drying out, then let rest at room temperature until the dough has roughly doubled in size, about 2 hours.

5. Preheat the oven to 425°F / 220°C.

6. Use your fingers to create deep dimples in the dough. Scatter the remaining 3 tablespoons chopped sun-dried tomatoes over the top, pressing them into the dough slightly to prevent burning.

7. Bake for 16 to 20 minutes, until golden.

8. Sprinkle with flaky sea salt while still warm. Let the muffins cool in the pan for 5 minutes, then run a knife around the edges to pop them out. Transfer to a wire rack to cool completely.

Charred Jalapeño & Green Onion Dip

Makes about 2 cups — Prep: 15 minutes Cook: 10 minutes Total: 25 minutes

This dip came to life after we tossed a few jalapeños and green onions on the grill during a summer cookout. The smoky flavor was so good, I couldn't stop thinking of more ways to use it. Even with the grill tucked away, I kept charring them in a skillet instead. So far, my favorite way to use them has been in this dip, chopped up and folded into a creamy, savory cream cheese base. It's simple, full of flavor, and perfect with crackers, fresh veggies, or spread into sandwiches. It's the kind of dip that disappears fast. Great for gatherings or, honestly, just for yourself with a good show lined up.

3 jalapeños
4 green onions, halved crosswise
1 tablespoon vegetable oil
1¼ cups / 285g vegan cream cheese
¼ cup / 60g vegan mayonnaise
2 tablespoons nutritional yeast flakes
Juice of ½ lime
1 teaspoon Mexican seasoning or taco seasoning
1 teaspoon white miso paste
Pinch of freshly ground black pepper

OPTIONAL GARNISHES

Fresh cilantro
Vegan bacon bits
Shredded vegan cheese
Sliced fresh jalapeño

1. Brush the jalapeños and green onions with the oil.
2. Heat a large cast-iron skillet or grill pan over high heat and add the vegetables in a single layer. Turn the jalapeños occasionally until they are lightly charred and blistered on all sides. Remove the green onions as they char, which may take 2 to 3 minutes. The jalapeños will take 8 to 10 minutes.
3. When cool enough to handle, finely chop the jalapeños (discard the seeds) and green onions and transfer to a large bowl. If you like, set aside a few grilled onion pieces to garnish the dip later.
4. Add the cream cheese, mayo, nutritional yeast, lime juice, Mexican seasoning, miso, and black pepper. Mix until smooth and well combined.
5. Spoon into a serving bowl and top with any or all of the garnishes and the reserved grilled onion pieces, if desired.

Roasted Patatas Bravas

with Simple Aioli

Serves 4 — Prep: 20 minutes Cook: 45 minutes Total: 1 hour 5 minutes

The first time I had patatas bravas was at a tiny bar tucked alongside a bustling plaza in Alicante. We were fresh off the plane and ordered them on a whim with a bowl of olives (I'm never not ordering olives). One bite in, and I was obsessed. Since then, anytime we visit Spain, if we're sitting on a terrace, we always order a plate to share.

Patatas bravas literally means "fierce potatoes," and they're one of Spain's most iconic tapas. While the potatoes are traditionally deep-fried, this version takes the oven-crunchy route instead. A quick parboil and a shake in the pot create a rough exterior, so they roast up beautifully crispy on the outside. They're finished with a bold, smoky brava sauce and a simple aioli. Simple, satisfying, and always a hit.

CRISPY POTATOES

8 medium Yukon Gold potatoes (2¼ pounds / 1kg total), peeled, cut into ½-inch / 1cm chunks

1 tablespoon plus 1 teaspoon fine sea salt

¼ teaspoon baking soda

2 tablespoons olive oil

BRAVA SAUCE

½ tablespoon olive oil

½ tablespoon smoked paprika

⅛ teaspoon cayenne pepper

2 tablespoons tomato paste

¾ cup / 180g canned crushed tomatoes

1 teaspoon sugar

⅛ teaspoon fine sea salt

¼ teaspoon red wine vinegar

SIMPLE AIOLI

½ cup / 120g vegan mayonnaise

2 garlic cloves, crushed to a paste

Juice of ½ lemon

¼ teaspoon fine sea salt

1. **MAKE THE CRISPY POTATOES:** Place the potatoes, 1 tablespoon of the salt, and the baking soda in a large pot filled with water and bring to a boil. Reduce to a simmer and cook for about 15 minutes, or until the potatoes are tender.

2. Preheat the oven to 425°F / 220°C. Line a baking sheet with parchment paper.

3. Drain the potatoes and return to the pot. Pour in the oil and sprinkle with the remaining 1 teaspoon salt, then cover with a lid and shake for a few seconds to create a rough exterior.

4. Spread the potatoes out on the prepared baking sheet and roast until golden and crunchy, 40 to 45 minutes, flipping them halfway through.

5. **MAKE THE BRAVA SAUCE:** In a medium skillet, heat the oil over medium-high heat. Stir in the smoked paprika and cayenne and toast for 30 seconds, stirring constantly. Mix in the tomato paste and cook, stirring often, for about 3 minutes, or until it darkens in color.

6. Pour in the crushed tomatoes, sugar, and salt. Simmer uncovered, stirring often, for about 10 minutes, or until thickened and rich in color. Remove from the heat and stir in the vinegar.

7. **MAKE THE SIMPLE AIOLI:** In a small bowl, stir together the mayo, garlic, lemon juice, and salt.

8. To serve, arrange the oven-roasted potatoes on a platter and add dollops of brava sauce and the aioli on top.

SOVRINTENDENTE AL

Balsamic Nectarine Crostini

Serves 6 — Prep: 20 minutes Cook: 20 minutes Total: 40 minutes

Versions of this crostini are all over the internet, often topped with burrata or whipped feta. This plant-based take swaps in a creamy tofu and cashew spread that's rich, tangy, and just a little umami, then gets finished with a drizzle of balsamic reduction and a handful of torn basil. It's quick to pull together but still feels special, especially for summer gatherings.

1 cup / 130g raw cashews

1 large ciabatta loaf (about 1 pound / 455g), sliced ½ inch / 1cm thick

Olive oil

3 nectarines, sliced

3½ ounces / 100g firm tofu

Juice of 1 lemon

1½ tablespoons nutritional yeast flakes

1 tablespoon white miso paste

½ teaspoon onion powder

¼ teaspoon fine sea salt

3 tablespoons balsamic reduction

¼ cup / 4g fresh basil leaves, thinly sliced

1. Preheat the oven to 400°F / 200°C. Line a wire rack with parchment paper.

2. In a heatproof medium bowl, cover the cashews with plenty of boiling water and let sit for 10 minutes to soften.

3. Arrange the sliced ciabatta on the lined rack and brush both sides of each slice with olive oil (about 2 tablespoons oil total). Transfer to the oven.

4. Bake for 8 to 10 minutes, until golden and crisp.

5. Meanwhile, in a cast-iron skillet or grill pan, heat about 2 teaspoons olive oil over medium-high heat. Grill the nectarine slices in a single layer until lightly charred on both sides, about 2 minutes per side.

6. Drain the cashews and transfer them to a food processor along with the tofu, lemon juice, nutritional yeast, miso, onion powder, salt, and ½ tablespoon olive oil. Blend until smooth.

7. Spread the cashew cheese onto the toasted bread. Top with grilled nectarines and a drizzle of balsamic reduction. Top with the fresh basil and serve.

HEADS-UP: Add the balsamic reduction just before serving to keep the bread from going soft.

Mediterranean "Cheese" Balls

Makes 2 cheese balls — Prep: 20 minutes Cook: 0 minutes Total: 20 minutes

My father-in-law is not plant-based, but I've always appreciated his willingness to try the plant-based creations we make. I never quite know how they'll be received, and when I served this cheese ball—a savory, spreadable blend of beans and cashews, packed with briny olives and sun-dried tomatoes—I made sure to include a few other familiar dips and crackers we knew he liked. He was helping us build our baby room at the time, and during one of our snack breaks, he spread some of this "cheese" onto a cracker, took a bite, looked over at me with wide eyes and said, "You made this?" then gave me an ecstatic thumbs up and the biggest smile. The familiar dips were barely touched, and the cheese ball disappeared in no time. That felt like a win to me.

- 1 cup / 180g canned cannellini beans, drained and rinsed
- 1 cup / 130g raw cashews
- 1 tablespoon nutritional yeast flakes
- 1 tablespoon tomato paste
- 2 tablespoons plus 2 teaspoons dried oregano
- 1 teaspoon garlic powder
- ¼ teaspoon fine sea salt
- ⅓ cup / 45g pitted kalamata olives, finely chopped
- ¼ cup / 38g oil-packed sun-dried tomatoes, drained and minced
- ⅓ cup / 15g dried onion flakes or finely chopped parsley
- Crackers, veggies, and fruits, for serving

1. In a food processor, combine the beans, cashews, nutritional yeast, tomato paste, 2 teaspoons of the oregano, the garlic powder, and salt. Blend until smooth. Remove the blades, then fold in the chopped olives and sun-dried tomatoes.

2. In a medium bowl, mix together the onion flakes and the remaining 2 tablespoons oregano.

3. Divide the "cheese" mixture in half and use your hands to shape each portion into a ball. Roll each ball in the onion/oregano mixture until fully coated.

4. Serve alongside crackers, veggies, and fruits.

Baked Jalapeño Poppers

Makes 12 poppers — Prep: 20 minutes Cook: 25 minutes Total: 45 minutes

The first time I had jalapeño poppers, I was a teenager visiting my cousin in California. We picked some up at a drive-through, breaded, deep-fried, and stuffed with cheese. To be honest, they were a bit too rich for me. But years later, out of the blue, I found myself craving them. So we set out to make a baked, plant-based version that still hit all the right notes: creamy, crispy, and just the right amount of spicy, but with a wholesome twist. My husband was skeptical about eating an entire jalapeño half at first, but after trying one, he nearly polished off the entire batch on his own. They are perfect for parties, but just as satisfying when you are in the mood for a snack you don't have to share.

- 6 jalapeños
- ½ cup / 90g canned cannellini beans
- 2 teaspoons minced canned chipotle peppers in adobo sauce
- ¼ cup / 41g corn kernels, canned or thawed frozen
- 2 tablespoons refined coconut oil, melted
- ½ tablespoon nutritional yeast flakes
- 2 teaspoons apple cider vinegar
- ¾ teaspoon fine sea salt
- ¼ cup / 14g panko bread crumbs
- 2 teaspoons taco seasoning
- Cooking spray, as needed
- Chopped fresh chives (optional), for garnish

1. Preheat the oven to 350°F / 180°C. Line a baking sheet with parchment paper.
2. Halve the jalapeños and remove the seeds and membranes.
3. In a medium bowl, mash the beans and chipotle together with a fork. Stir in the corn, 1 tablespoon of the coconut oil, the nutritional yeast, vinegar, and ½ teaspoon of the salt.
4. Divide the filling among the jalapeño halves.
5. In a small bowl, mix together the panko, taco seasoning, and the remaining 1 tablespoon coconut oil and ¼ teaspoon salt.
6. Sprinkle the panko mixture over the filled jalapeños, gently pressing it down to help it stick. Arrange the jalapeño halves on the prepared baking sheet and spritz with cooking spray. Transfer to the oven.
7. Bake for 20 to 25 minutes, until the topping is golden.
8. Serve garnished with chopped chives, if desired.

Mutabbal

(Roasted Eggplant Dip)

Makes about 2 cups — **Prep:** 10 minutes **Cook:** 35 minutes **Total:** 45 minutes

Mutabbal is a creamy eggplant dip from the Levantine region of the Middle East, often mistaken for baba ghanoush. The two are close cousins, both eggplant-based, but traditionally quite different. Mutabbal is made with tahini, garlic, lemon juice, and spices (and sometimes yogurt for a creamier, tangier dip). Baba ghanoush, on the other hand, is flavored with pomegranate molasses and originally didn't include tahini at all. Over time, though, the lines have blurred. These days, many baba ghanoush recipes include tahini, and the two have become something of a hybrid in modern kitchens. Still, I always prefer mutabbal. The earthiness of the tahini with the smokiness of eggplant is such a delicious match. While mutabbal is traditionally made with fire-roasted eggplant, this version uses the oven to keep it easy and approachable.

4 medium eggplants (2½ pounds / 1.1kg total)

¼ cup / 60ml lemon juice (about 2 lemons)

1 garlic clove, crushed to a paste

½ cup / 130g tahini (see Heads-Up)

2 tablespoons extra-virgin olive oil

2 tablespoons unsweetened soy or almond yogurt (optional)

1 teaspoon ground cumin

1 teaspoon fine sea salt, plus more to taste

2 tablespoons chopped fresh parsley (optional), for garnish

½ tablespoon za'atar spice mix (optional), for garnish

1. Preheat the oven to 425°F / 220°C. Line a baking sheet with parchment paper.

2. Cut the eggplants lengthwise and place them cut-side down on the prepared baking sheet. Poke several times with a fork and transfer to the oven.

3. Bake for 35 to 40 minutes, until the eggplants are fully softened.

4. Set a fine-mesh sieve over a large bowl. When the eggplants are cool enough to handle, scoop the eggplant flesh into the sieve (discard the skins). Use the back of the spoon to press out some of the liquid from the eggplant—you only want to extract the liquid that easily pours out when pressed, usually about ¾ cup / 180ml; it's okay if some liquid remains, no need to press it super dry.

5. Discard the liquid and transfer the eggplant to the empty bowl. Use a fork to mash the eggplant until it becomes smooth. Add the lemon juice, garlic, tahini, olive oil, yogurt (if using), cumin, and salt. Mash again with the fork until well combined. Taste and add more salt if you like.

6. Transfer to a serving bowl. If desired, garnish with parsley and za'atar, and serve with warm pita bread or fresh veggies.

HEADS-UP: Preferably choose a tahini made from roasted sesame seeds. The roasted kind has a more intense nutty flavor and a golden hue (which makes the dip super delicious!) whereas raw tahini is milder and paler in color (and milder in taste).

Caramelized Onion Jam Pinwheels

Makes 12 pinwheels — Prep: 20 minutes Cook: 1 hour Total: 1 hour 20 minutes

I've never met a caramelized onion recipe I didn't love, and this one might be my all-time favorite. The sweet, jammy onions melt into a creamy tofu and cashew filling, all wrapped in golden puff pastry that bakes to crispy perfection. It's a mix of sweet and savory, perfect for sharing, but it's also guaranteed that you'll want to keep them all to yourself.

RED ONION JAM

2 tablespoons olive oil

2 small red onions (about 15 ounces / 425g total), thinly sliced

3 tablespoons sugar

¼ cup / 60ml balsamic vinegar

¼ teaspoon fine sea salt

TOFU CASHEW FILLING

¼ cup / 33g raw cashews

3½ ounces / 100g firm tofu

1 teaspoon dried parsley

1 teaspoon dried chives

½ teaspoon garlic powder

½ teaspoon fine sea salt

ASSEMBLY

Olive oil, for the muffin tin

2 tablespoons bread crumbs

9½ ounces / 270g vegan puff pastry dough, thawed if frozen

1. **MAKE THE ONION JAM:** In a large skillet, heat the oil over medium-high heat. Add the onions and cook for 10 minutes, or until lightly caramelized.

2. Reduce the heat to low and sprinkle the sugar over the onions. Let it cook undisturbed for 5 minutes to allow the sugar to melt evenly. Then stir to combine.

3. Add the vinegar and salt, and stir again. Raise the heat to medium to bring the mixture to a gentle simmer and cook for 7 to 8 minutes, until the mixture thickens into a jam-like consistency. Set aside to cool slightly.

4. **MAKE THE TOFU CASHEW FILLING:** In a small food processor, blend the cashews until crumbly. Add the tofu, parsley, chives, garlic powder, and salt. Blend until smooth.

5. **ASSEMBLE THE ROLLS:** Preheat the oven to 400°F / 200°C. Generously grease 12 cups of a standard muffin tin and sprinkle the bread crumbs into the bottom of each muffin cup. Don't skip the bread crumbs, as they prevent the rolls from sticking once baked.

6. Roll out the puff pastry into a rectangle measuring about 10 × 12 inches / 25 × 30cm.

7. With a long side facing you, spread the tofu filling evenly over the rectangle, then spoon and spread the onion jam on top. Starting on the long side, roll up the pastry tightly into a log. Cut crosswise into 12 even pieces and place each into a prepared muffin cup and transfer to the oven.

8. Bake for about 30 minutes, or until golden and crisp.

9. Let the pinwheels cool slightly in the pan, then transfer to a wire rack to cool completely.

HEADS-UP: Even if you're not up for making the full recipe, the onion jam is worth making on its own. It's perfect on a snack board with crackers or spooned over grilled veggies or baked tofu.

Baked Korean Cauliflower Wings

Serves 4 — Prep: 20 minutes Cook: 30 minutes Total: 50 minutes

This recipe was inspired by the Korean cauliflower wings on our app. That version is deep-fried, but after so many of you asked for a lighter option, we got to work. The result is tender cauliflower bites coated in a sticky, finger-licking sauce that hits just the right balance of sweet and heat, thanks to a bold gochujang base. We adjusted a few ingredients to make sure everything roasts up just right in the oven—no frying required. Perfect as an appetizer, party snack, or for game nights and movie marathons alike.

CAULIFLOWER WINGS

½ cup plus 1 tablespoon / 135ml water

½ cup / 70g all-purpose flour

½ tablespoon onion powder

1 teaspoon smoked paprika

1 medium head cauliflower (1⅓ pounds / 620g total), cut into large florets

1½ cups / 85g panko bread crumbs

Cooking spray

GOCHUJANG GLAZE

2 tablespoons toasted sesame oil

2 garlic cloves, minced

1 teaspoon grated fresh ginger

2½ tablespoons agave or maple syrup

2 tablespoons gochujang

2 tablespoons reduced-sodium soy sauce

1 tablespoon rice vinegar

1. **PREPARE THE CAULIFLOWER WINGS:** Preheat the oven to 425°F / 220°C. Line two baking sheets with parchment paper.
2. In a large bowl, whisk together the water, flour, onion powder, and smoked paprika until smooth. Add the cauliflower and toss to coat evenly in the batter.
3. Place the panko in a shallow bowl. Working with one piece at a time, dip the battered cauliflower into the panko, pressing gently to help the crumbs stick. Arrange the coated cauliflower on the prepared baking sheets. Spritz generously with cooking spray and transfer to the oven.
4. Bake until golden, 20 to 25 minutes, flipping the pieces and rotating the sheets front to back halfway through.
5. **MAKE THE GOCHUJANG GLAZE:** In a small pan, heat ½ tablespoon of the sesame oil over medium heat. Add the garlic and ginger and cook for about 2 minutes, or until fragrant.
6. Transfer the garlic and ginger to a large bowl. Add the agave, gochujang, soy sauce, vinegar, and the remaining 1½ tablespoons sesame oil and stir to combine.
7. Once the cauliflower is baked, toss it in the glaze until well coated, then return the pieces to the baking sheets. Return to the oven and bake for 5 to 7 minutes, until the glaze is set and slightly caramelized.
8. Serve warm, shortly after removing from the oven.

Sides

Spicy Garlic Tofu

FAN FAVORITE

Serves 4 — Prep: 15 minutes Cook: 20 minutes Total: 35 minutes

If you'd asked me years ago if tofu could be addictive, I would've laughed. But this recipe changed that for me, and judging by the hundreds of five-star reviews for this recipe on our website, I'm not alone. It transforms humble tofu into something bold, flavorful, and downright irresistible, perfect for tossing into a stir-fry or piling over rice. Even the skeptics have come around. One reader said her husband took one bite and said, "If you can get me to eat tofu, it's good." That pretty much says it all.

- **14 ounces / 395g firm tofu,** pressed (see How to Press Tofu, page 37) and cut into ½-inch / 1cm cubes
- **1½ tablespoons cornstarch**
- **¼ teaspoon fine sea salt**
- **⅛ teaspoon freshly ground black pepper**
- **3 tablespoons vegetable oil**
- **2 tablespoons maple syrup**
- **1 tablespoon gochujang**
- **1 tablespoon reduced-sodium soy sauce**
- **1 tablespoon rice vinegar**
- **5 garlic cloves,** minced
- **1 medium shallot,** finely chopped
- **2 fresh red chiles,** thinly sliced
- **2 green onions,** thinly sliced, plus more for garnish
- **Toasted sesame seeds (optional),** for garnish

1. Place the tofu cubes in a large bowl. Add the cornstarch, salt, and black pepper and gently toss to coat.

2. In a large skillet, heat 1 tablespoon of the oil over medium-high heat. Cook the tofu for 8 to 10 minutes, until golden. Try to not disturb the tofu too much to avoid crumbling.

3. Meanwhile, in a small bowl, mix together the maple syrup, gochujang, soy sauce, and rice vinegar. Set aside.

4. When the tofu is crisped to your liking, transfer it to a plate. In the same pan over medium-high heat, drizzle in the remaining 2 tablespoons oil. When hot, add the garlic, shallot, chiles, and green onions and cook for about 4 minutes, or until golden.

5. Reduce the heat to medium and add the sauce, cooking for 2 to 3 minutes, until the sauce becomes sticky. Add the tofu to the pan and stir to coat.

6. Transfer to a plate and garnish with some sliced green onions and sesame seeds (if using).

Tamarind-Glazed Zucchini with Cashew Mint Chutney

Serves 6 — Prep: 30 minutes Cook: 20 minutes Total: 50 minutes

My sisters always say you can't open our mom's fridge without spotting at least one jar of herby homemade chutney. I didn't fully appreciate it as a kid, but now I see how much a good chutney can do. It adds freshness, acidity, and brings a dish to life. In this side dish, curry spiced zucchini is grilled until charred and tender (I like using a mix of green and yellow for a bit more color), then finished with two bold sauces: a sticky, tangy sweet tamarind glaze and a creamy mint cashew chutney inspired by dear Mum.

GRILLED ZUCCHINI

3 large zucchini (about 2.1 pounds / 965g total)
1½ tablespoons olive oil
1 tablespoon curry powder
¼ teaspoon fine sea salt

CASHEW MINT CHUTNEY

1 cup / 16g fresh cilantro
½ cup / 70g unsalted roasted cashews
¼ cup / 4g fresh mint leaves
1 jalapeño, seeded
1 garlic clove, peeled but whole
Juice of 1 lime
2 tablespoons extra-virgin olive oil
2 tablespoons water
¼ teaspoon ground cumin
¼ teaspoon fine sea salt

TAMARIND GLAZE

2 tablespoons tamarind paste
2 tablespoons maple syrup

TOPPINGS

¼ small red onion, thinly sliced
½ jalapeño, thinly sliced
¼ cup / 34g unsalted roasted cashews, chopped

1. **GRILL THE ZUCCHINI:** Slice the zucchini lengthwise into planks ½ inch / 1cm thick. Then halve them crosswise and transfer to a large bowl. Drizzle with the olive oil and sprinkle with curry powder and salt. Toss to coat.

2. Preheat a grill or grill pan to medium heat. Add the zucchini planks in a single layer and grill until there are char marks, about 3 minutes per side.

3. **MAKE THE CASHEW MINT CHUTNEY:** In a small food processor, combine the cilantro, cashews, mint, jalapeño, garlic, lime juice, olive oil, water, cumin, and salt. Blend and set aside.

4. **MAKE THE TAMARIND GLAZE:** In a small bowl, stir together the tamarind paste and maple syrup (see Heads-Up).

5. Transfer the grilled zucchini to a large serving plate. Very lightly brush the tamarind glaze over the warm zucchini, then dollop any remaining glaze on top. Dollop over the chutney. Top with the red onion, jalapeño, and chopped cashews.

HEADS-UP: There are plenty of different tamarind products on the market. The one we used is a thick, seedless paste made from 100% tamarind, no other added ingredients. It's very sour on its own, so a splash of maple syrup helps balance it out beautifully.

Harissa Maple Glazed Roasted Carrots

Serves 4 — Prep: 10 minutes Cook: 30 minutes Total: 40 minutes

I have to admit, I've been gatekeeping this recipe for over four years. I always knew that when the day came to write a cookbook, this one had to be in it. It's wonderfully simple yet surprisingly sophisticated. The humble carrot gets transformed with a harissa-maple glaze that's spicy, sweet, and zesty, and then layered over a cool, creamy base of coconut yogurt. What I love most is the contrast: hot and cold, spicy and mellow. It looks gorgeous on the table and tastes even better.

3 tablespoons olive oil
3 tablespoons maple syrup
2 tablespoons fresh lemon juice
1 tablespoon harissa paste
½ teaspoon ground cumin
¼ teaspoon ground cinnamon
¼ teaspoon fine sea salt
⅛ teaspoon freshly ground black pepper
10 thin carrots (1 pound 6 ounces / 630g), peeled
½ cup / 120ml unsweetened coconut yogurt
4 small radishes (optional), sliced
3 tablespoons unsalted roasted almonds, chopped (see Heads-Up)
1 tablespoon fresh mint leaves, thinly sliced

1. Preheat the oven to 425°F / 220°C.

2. In a small bowl, mix together the oil, maple syrup, lemon juice, harissa paste, cumin, cinnamon, salt, and pepper. Measure out 1 tablespoon of the harissa maple glaze and set aside for garnish.

3. Place the carrots in a single layer in a large baking dish. Pour the rest of the glaze over the carrots and toss to coat. Cover the dish with a lid or foil and transfer to the oven.

4. Roast for 15 minutes. Toss, then bake uncovered for another 15 minutes, or until the carrots are tender with a slight bite. Thinner carrots will cook more quickly, and thicker carrots will take longer to cook.

5. Spread the coconut yogurt across a serving platter, top with the warm carrots, radish slices (if using), and the reserved harissa mixture. Spoon any remaining harissa marinade from the baking dish over the top as well. Finish with a sprinkle of almonds and mint.

HEADS-UP: The almonds add a lovely crunch, but if you're looking to dress things up, a sprinkle of dukkah makes it extra special. Try it if you have some on hand.

Sambal Green Beans

Serves 4 — Prep: 10 minutes Cook: 15 minutes Total: 25 minutes

I don't say this lightly, but this one has *never* made it to leftovers. This is my go-to side dish when I need something quick that looks far more impressive and sophisticated than the effort it takes to make it. It brings back memories of the rich flavors of Indonesia, with green beans stir-fried to tender-crisp perfection and coated in a glossy sambal sauce.

1 tablespoon vegetable oil

1 medium shallot, thinly sliced

1 pound / 455g green beans, ends trimmed

2 garlic cloves, thinly sliced

5 dried red chiles (optional)

2 tablespoons water

¼ cup / 37g salted roasted peanuts, chopped

2 tablespoons reduced-sodium soy sauce

1 tablespoon light brown sugar

1 tablespoon sambal oelek

1 tablespoon toasted sesame oil

Fresh cilantro (optional), for garnish

Crispy fried shallots (optional), for garnish

1. In a large sauté pan, heat the oil over medium-high heat until hot. Add the shallot and cook for 3 minutes, or until lightly golden.
2. Add the green beans, garlic, dried chiles (if using), and water and stir. Cover and steam for 5 to 6 minutes, until the beans are bright green and slightly softened.
3. Uncover and add the peanuts, soy sauce, brown sugar, sambal, and sesame oil. Cook for 2 to 3 minutes more, until the beans reach your desired tenderness.
4. Serve as is, or with one or both of the garnishes, if desired.

Grilled Portobellos
with Chermoula Sauce

Serves 4 — Prep: 20 minutes Cook: 15 minutes Total: 35 minutes

There are sides that complement a meal, and then there are sides that demand attention and outshine the main. This is one of those. Juicy, meaty, and rich in umami, these grilled portobello mushrooms are hearty enough to win over even the most devoted meat-lovers.

It's a recipe I find myself making every summer when my husband fires up the grill—though it's just as easy to make in a grill pan or skillet year-round. Topped with an herby chermoula sauce—a zesty North African marinade made from fresh herbs, garlic, spices, and lemon—they're always the first thing to disappear at a BBQ.

CHERMOULA SAUCE

1 garlic clove, crushed to a paste

Grated zest and juice of ½ lemon

⅓ cup / 80ml extra-virgin olive oil

¼ cup / 4g fresh parsley, finely chopped

¼ cup / 4g fresh cilantro, finely chopped

¼ teaspoon chile flakes

¼ teaspoon ground coriander

¼ teaspoon ground cumin

¼ teaspoon fine sea salt

⅛ teaspoon smoked paprika

GRILLED MUSHROOMS

8 portobello mushrooms

¼ cup / 60ml olive oil

¼ teaspoon fine sea salt

¼ teaspoon freshly ground black pepper

1. Preheat a grill or grill pan to medium-high heat.

2. **MAKE THE CHERMOULA SAUCE:** In a small bowl, stir together the garlic, lemon zest, lemon juice, extra-virgin olive oil, parsley, cilantro, chile flakes, coriander, cumin, salt, and paprika. Set aside.

3. **GRILL THE MUSHROOMS:** Place the mushrooms in a large bowl and generously brush each with oil. Sprinkle them with the salt and pepper.

4. Set the mushrooms on the grill, cover, and cook until softened and lightly charred on both sides, about 4 minutes per side. (If cooking in a grill pan, add a small splash of water to the pan before covering with a lid.)

5. Brush the top sides of the mushrooms with some of the chermoula sauce. Don't flip the mushrooms, but cover and grill for another 2 minutes.

6. Flip the mushrooms over and brush the bottom sides with chermoula, cover, and grill for another 2 minutes.

7. Arrange the mushrooms on a plate and drizzle with the remaining chermoula sauce, or serve it on the side.

HEADS-UP: The chermoula is worth making on its own. Drizzle it over roasted veggies, spoon it onto nourish bowls, or keep a jar in the fridge to jazz up whatever you're cooking.

Sautéed Broccolini
with Whipped Tahini

Serves 3 or 4 — Prep: 10 minutes Cook: 20 minutes Total: 30 minutes

I often joke that food, for me, is just a carrying device for sauce—the saucier the dish, the better. And this whipped tahini sauce, which serves as the base for tender sautéed broccolini, is one I'd happily lick off the plate. No shame. As always, I recommend using a tahini made from roasted sesame seeds rather than raw sesame seeds for a richer flavor.

WHIPPED TAHINI

1½ tablespoons vegetable oil
1 medium shallot, finely chopped
1 garlic clove, minced
Juice of ½ lemon
¼ cup / 65g tahini
1 teaspoon agave syrup
Pinch of fine sea salt
3 tablespoons water

SAUTÉED BROCCOLINI

1½ tablespoons vegetable oil
8 ounces / 225g broccolini (about 2 small bunches), ends trimmed
¼ teaspoon fine sea salt
⅓ cup / 80ml water
¼ teaspoon chile flakes
Toasted sesame seeds (optional), for garnish

1. **MAKE THE WHIPPED TAHINI:** In a medium skillet, heat the oil over medium heat until hot. Add the shallot and garlic and cook for 3 to 5 minutes, until golden.

2. Transfer this shallot-garlic mixture to a tall jar (that can fit an immersion blender). Add the lemon juice, tahini, agave syrup, and salt. Use an immersion blender to blend the ingredients until smooth. Gradually add the water 1 tablespoon at a time, blending after each addition until the mixture becomes creamy and reaches a pourable consistency. Set aside. (Alternatively, blend in a small food processor.)

3. **SAUTÉ THE BROCCOLINI:** In the skillet that the shallots and garlic were cooked in, heat the oil over medium heat until hot. Add the broccolini and salt and cook for 3 to 4 minutes, until seared and bright green.

4. Pour in the water, cover, and steam until the thickest parts of the stalk are tender, about 8 minutes. Uncover and sprinkle the broccolini with the chile flakes.

5. Spread the whipped tahini onto a serving platter, then arrange the broccolini on top. Serve warm, sprinkled with toasted sesame seeds (if using).

Jeweled Rice

Serves 6 —— Prep: 20 minutes Cook: 30 minutes Total: 50 minutes

This recipe brings back the flavors of my childhood in a single dish. Jeweled rice, a traditional Persian recipe, is known for its rich aroma, golden saffron hue, and the sparkle of dried fruits and nuts scattered over top like little edible gems. Traditionally, it's a bit of a project, taking time, care, and more pots than I usually feel like washing. But this simplified take delivers all the magic with far less fuss.

The aroma alone is worth it—buttery, floral, spiced—the kind that lingers and makes your whole home smell incredible. One of our recipe developers put it best: "Gosh, cooking this really did fill my kitchen with the most gorgeous scent—someone should bottle it up or turn it into a fancy candle!" She's not wrong.

- 20 saffron threads (½ to 1 teaspoon loosely packed)
- 3 tablespoons hot water
- 1½ cups / 300g basmati rice
- 10 cups / 2.4L water
- 1½ tablespoons plus ½ teaspoon fine sea salt
- 2½ tablespoons unsalted vegan butter
- 2 medium onions, diced
- ⅓ cup / 43g dried apricots, finely chopped
- ⅓ cup / 48g dried cranberries, or ¼ cup / 20g dried barberries
- ¼ cup / 55g raisins
- ½ teaspoon ground cumin
- ¼ teaspoon ground cinnamon
- ⅛ teaspoon ground cardamom
- ⅛ teaspoon ground allspice (optional)
- ¼ cup / 23g toasted sliced almonds
- ¼ cup / 31g unsalted roasted pistachios, chopped

1. Grind the saffron in a mortar and pestle. Add the hot water and set aside.
2. Rinse the rice multiple times until the water runs clear.
3. In a large pot, bring the water and 1½ tablespoons of the salt to a boil.
4. Add the rice, cover, and cook for 10 to 12 minutes, until soft but still slightly al dente (it will continue cooking in later steps). Drain the rice in a colander, then return the rice to the pot. Set aside.
5. Meanwhile, in a large heavy-bottomed sauté pan, melt 1 tablespoon of the butter over medium-high heat. Add the onions and the remaining ½ teaspoon salt and cook for about 5 minutes, or until golden.
6. Stir in the apricots, cranberries, raisins, cumin, cinnamon, cardamom, and allspice (if using). Cook for an extra minute to toast the spices.
7. Transfer the mixture to the rice and gently fold to combine.
8. Wipe out the sauté pan, then melt the remaining 1½ tablespoons butter over medium heat. Add the rice mixture and drizzle the saffron water over the rice. Cover and cook for about 5 minutes, or until the bottom layer of rice turns lightly golden and crisp.
9. To serve, transfer to a plate and garnish with the almonds and pistachios.

Buttery Sage Potatoes

Serves 4 — Prep: 10 minutes Cook: 25 minutes Total: 35 minutes

You tell me, is there any side dish that disappears faster than a plate of perfectly seasoned, golden potatoes? Nope. Nope, there isn't. And this potato side is no exception. Infused with the richness of butter and fragrant, aromatic sage, this side is simple to make and flavor-packed, and it pairs perfectly with just about anything.

1 pound / 455g baby potatoes, halved

Fine sea salt

2 tablespoons unsalted vegan butter

½ tablespoon olive oil

30 fresh sage leaves, chopped

¾ teaspoon garlic powder

½ teaspoon onion powder

⅛ teaspoon freshly ground black pepper

OPTIONAL GARNISHES

Fried sage leaves (see Heads-Up)

Chile flakes

Flaky sea salt

1. Place the potatoes in a large pot of generously salted water. Bring to a gentle simmer and cook for 15 to 18 minutes, until the potatoes are tender. Drain.

2. In a large sauté pan, melt the butter over medium-high heat and add the oil. Once hot, add the chopped sage and cook until lightly crispy and fragrant, 1 to 2 minutes.

3. Add the drained potatoes to the pan along with the garlic powder, onion powder, ¼ teaspoon salt, and the pepper. Cook, stirring frequently, for 8 to 10 minutes, until the potatoes are golden.

4. Plate the buttery sage potatoes. If desired, top with any or all of the garnishes.

HEADS-UP: For a little extra flair, you can add an optional fried sage leaf garnish. Fry 16 fresh sage leaves in ¼ cup / 60ml olive oil over medium-high heat for 30 to 60 seconds, or until the edges stop bubbling. Transfer to paper towels to drain.

Vegan Garlic Naan

FAN FAVORITE

Makes 4 naan — Prep: 20 minutes Cook: 10 minutes Total: 30 minutes

Oh, naan. The ultimate curry companion. While many store-bought versions aren't vegan (and often fall a little flat), homemade naan is on a whole other level—soft, warm, and full of flavor. This version has become a fan favorite for good reason: no yeast, no rising time, just quick, reliable results every time.

While plain naan is great, my favorite has always been garlic naan—it packs so much more flavor and makes whatever it's served with taste that much better. Honestly, the hardest part is not eating it as soon as it comes off the pan. If you're anything like me, just go ahead and make more than you think you need. As one reader put it: "Super delicious! The only thing that I regret is that I haven't made a double batch!" You've been warned.

- 1½ tablespoons melted vegan butter or vegetable oil
- 2 garlic cloves, crushed to a paste
- ¾ teaspoon fine sea salt
- 2 cups / 270g all-purpose flour, plus more for dusting
- ½ cup / 130g unsweetened soy or almond yogurt
- ¼ cup / 60ml unsweetened soy or almond milk
- ½ tablespoon sugar
- 2 teaspoons baking powder
- ½ cup / 8g fresh cilantro, finely chopped

1. In a small bowl, combine the butter (or oil), garlic, and ½ teaspoon of the salt. Whisk and set aside.

2. In a large bowl, mix the flour, yogurt, milk, sugar, baking powder, and the remaining ¼ teaspoon salt until just combined.

3. Transfer the dough to a floured surface and knead until smooth. If it sticks to your hands or the surface, sprinkle with more flour as needed.

4. Divide the dough into 4 equal portions. Roll each piece into an oval shape, about 1⁄16 inch / 2mm thick, adding flour as needed to prevent sticking.

5. Preheat a large skillet (such as a cast-iron skillet) over medium-high heat.

6. Sprinkle some of the cilantro on one side of a naan and lightly roll over it with a rolling pin to help it stick. Flip the naan so the cilantro side is facing down, then lightly brush the top with water.

7. Place the naan, water-side down, into the hot pan and cook until bubbles form and the bottom is golden, about 1 minute. Flip the naan, quickly add 1 teaspoon water around the edge of the pan, cover, and steam until the bottom is golden, about 1 minute.

8. Uncover and reduce the heat to medium. Brush the top with the garlic butter. Flip and cook for 30 seconds, or until the garlic is fragrant and golden. Brush the top with more garlic butter, then flip and cook for another 30 seconds. Transfer to a plate and cover to keep warm.

9. Repeat with the remaining naan and garlic butter, wiping the skillet clean after each batch.

10. Serve warm (alongside your favorite curry).

Pastas & Noodles

Tofu Vermicelli Noodle Bowls with Peanut Sauce

Serves 2 — Prep: 30 minutes Cook: 20 minutes Total: 50 minutes

Inspired by Vietnamese vermicelli bowls, I crave this kind of meal on warm days: It's light and fresh, packed with herbs (the best part!), and drizzled with a creamy peanut sauce.

QUICK PICKLED VEGGIES

½ carrot, peeled and julienned

⅓ English cucumber, julienned

1 fresh Thai chile, thinly sliced

½ cup / 120ml rice vinegar

½ cup / 120ml boiling water

1 tablespoon maple syrup

TOFU

½ tablespoon vegetable oil

7 ounces / 200g firm tofu, pressed and cubed

1 tablespoon soy sauce

PEANUT DRESSING

¼ cup / 65g natural peanut butter

¼ cup / 60ml hot water

1½ tablespoons soy sauce

½ tablespoon rice vinegar

1 teaspoon maple syrup

1 garlic clove, crushed to a paste

ASSEMBLY

3.2 ounces / 90g rice vermicelli noodles

½ small head green leaf lettuce, chopped

¼ cup / 4g fresh mint leaves, thinly sliced

¼ cup / 4g fresh basil leaves, thinly sliced

Chopped salted roasted peanuts (optional), for topping

1. **MAKE THE QUICK PICKLED VEGGIES:** In a small jar, combine the carrot, cucumber, chile, vinegar, boiling water, and maple syrup. Cover with a lid and give it a good shake. Set aside.

2. **COOK THE TOFU:** In a large skillet, heat the oil over medium-high heat. Add the tofu and cook for about 8 minutes, or until golden. Turn off the heat and add the soy sauce. Stir quickly until absorbed, then remove from the heat to prevent burning.

3. **MAKE THE PEANUT DRESSING:** In a small bowl, mix together the peanut butter, hot water, soy sauce, vinegar, maple syrup, and garlic.

4. **ASSEMBLE THE BOWLS:** Cook the vermicelli noodles according to the package instructions. Drain the noodles, rinse under warm water, and divide them between serving bowls.

5. Top with the lettuce, fresh herbs, quick pickled veggies, and tofu. Drizzle with the peanut dressing and toss lightly. If desired, garnish with peanuts.

HEADS-UP: Got leftover tofu? Put it to good use in the Spinach Crêpes (page 50).

Sesame Udon Noodles
with Five-Spice Tofu Crumble

Serves 4 — Prep: 15 minutes Cook: 20 minutes Total: 35 minutes

It's a "how is it already 6 p.m.?" kind of recipe—the one I turn to when I want something as flavorful as takeout, but without spending all night in the kitchen. The udon noodles are thick and chewy, coated in a creamy, toasted sesame sauce. Crumbling tofu straight into the pan is one of the most satisfying parts—no need to cut it neatly. It cooks down into golden, savory bits that soak up dark soy sauce and five-spice beautifully, which gives it a surprisingly meat-like flavor. The chili crisp finishes this dish with some heat and crunch and should definitely not be skipped, but I'd recommend starting small to make sure it doesn't overpower the other flavors.

- 4 garlic cloves, minced
- 2 tablespoons Chinese sesame paste (see Heads-Up)
- 1½ tablespoons reduced-sodium soy sauce
- 2 tablespoons dark soy sauce
- 1 tablespoon light brown sugar
- 2 teaspoons rice vinegar
- 1½ tablespoons vegetable oil
- 14 ounces / 395g firm tofu, pressed (see How to Press Tofu, page 37)
- ¾ teaspoon five-spice powder
- 4 green onions, thinly sliced
- 12 ounces / 340g cremini mushrooms, sliced
- 1¾ pounds / 800g fresh udon noodles
- 2 tablespoons chili crisp, or to taste

1. In a small bowl, mix the garlic, sesame paste, reduced-sodium soy sauce, 1 tablespoon of the dark soy sauce, the brown sugar, and vinegar. Set the sesame sauce aside.

2. In a medium sauté pan, heat 1 tablespoon of the oil over medium-high heat. Crumble the tofu into the pan and cook for about 10 minutes, or until golden and crispy, stirring occasionally.

3. Add the remaining 1 tablespoon dark soy sauce and the five-spice powder and cook for 2 minutes more to toast. Transfer to a bowl and set aside.

4. Add the remaining ½ tablespoon oil to the now-empty sauté pan and heat over medium-high heat. Add the green onions and mushrooms and cook for about 4 minutes, or until lightly golden.

5. Cook the udon noodles according to the package instructions. Drain the udon and add to the sauté pan along with the sesame sauce. Cook for 2 minutes to reheat.

6. Serve the noodles in bowls and top with the tofu crumble and chili crisp.

HEADS-UP: I strongly recommend using Chinese sesame paste for this recipe, but if you can't find it, tahini works in a pinch. Just know the flavor will be milder. Ideally, use a dark roasted tahini (not the pale or raw kind) that more closely achieves the deep toasty richness that Chinese sesame paste offers.

One-Pot Golden Lemongrass Noodles

Serves 3 or 4 — **Prep:** 10 minutes **Cook:** 20 minutes **Total:** 30 minutes

This one-pot noodle dish is as creamy as it gets. Silken tofu gets blended right into the coconut milk, making the sauce extra smooth and giving it a subtle protein boost. The curry powder, turmeric, and ginger add warmth, depth, and a beautiful golden hue (plus a hit of antioxidants!). Just one thing to keep in mind: This is not a meal to prep ahead and come back to later. The noodles are delicate and will keep soaking up the sauce as they sit, so it's best served hot, right off the stove. Have your bowls ready—you'll want to dig in the second it's done.

1 tablespoon vegetable oil

3 garlic cloves, crushed to a paste

2 medium shallots, very thinly sliced

2 teaspoons grated fresh ginger

½ tablespoon lemongrass paste

1 tablespoon curry powder

2 teaspoons ground turmeric

1 (13.5-ounce / 400ml) can full-fat coconut milk

1 cup / 240ml water

½ tablespoon light brown sugar

½ teaspoon fine sea salt

¼ teaspoon cayenne pepper

⅛ teaspoon freshly ground black pepper

14 ounces / 400g silken tofu, roughly diced

8 ounces / 225g wide flat rice noodles

Juice of 1 lime

TOPPINGS

1½ tablespoons fried shallots

1½ tablespoons chili crisp

1 green onion, sliced

1. In a large pot, heat the oil over medium heat. Add the garlic, shallots, ginger, and lemongrass paste and cook for about 5 minutes, or until soft and fragrant.

2. Add the curry powder and turmeric and cook, stirring, for 1 minute to toast.

3. Add the coconut milk, water, brown sugar, salt, cayenne, black pepper, and just over three-quarters of the tofu. Reserve the remaining tofu cubes for garnish.

4. Use an immersion blender to blend until smooth. (Or blend in a countertop blender and return to the pot.)

5. Bring to a gentle boil, then add the noodles. Reduce the heat to maintain a gentle simmer and cook until the noodles are al dente according to the package instructions.

6. Squeeze in the lime juice—if you're sensitive to acidity, start with less and add more to taste.

7. Divide the noodles among serving bowls and top with the reserved tofu cubes and the toppings.

Bibim Guksu

(Spicy Korean Noodle Salad)

Serves 2 or 3 — Prep: 15 minutes Cook: 5 minutes Total: 20 minutes

I was first introduced to Korean food in high school, thanks to a few Korean friends who always knew the best spots to eat. We'd go out and share as many dishes as we could—hot pots, sizzling plates, and endless little bowls of banchan (Korean side dishes). That's when I discovered bibim guksu, and I've been obsessed ever since. It's usually enjoyed cold, and it's one of my go-to dishes during hot summer months: fresh and fiery, with chewy noodles, crunchy veggies, and a bright, tangy chile paste sauce. It also features kimchi—my all-time favorite Korean ingredient. I've more than once finished a small jar on its own with just chopsticks.

For this recipe, I recommend using somyeon or sōmen noodles, which can be found at most Asian grocery stores, though any thin wheat noodles should do.

- 1 garlic clove, minced
- 2 tablespoons gochujang
- 1½ tablespoons rice vinegar
- 1 tablespoon reduced-sodium soy sauce
- 1 tablespoon toasted sesame oil
- 1 tablespoon toasted sesame seeds
- 1 tablespoon light brown sugar
- 6.3 ounces / 180g thin wheat noodles
- 1 cup / 90g shredded green cabbage
- ½ English cucumber, cut into matchsticks
- ½ carrot, cut into matchsticks
- ⅔ cup / 105g cooked shelled edamame
- 3 tablespoons vegan kimchi, plus more to taste

1. In a small bowl, mix the garlic, gochujang, vinegar, soy sauce, sesame oil, sesame seeds, and brown sugar. Set aside.

2. Cook the noodles according to package instructions. Once done, drain, rinse under cold water, and place in a serving bowl.

3. Add the cabbage, cucumber, carrot, edamame, and kimchi and drizzle the sauce over top. Give everything a good toss to coat.

HEADS-UP: Kimchi is not always plant-based as it often includes seafood-based seasonings. Vegan versions are easy to find or make at home (we've got a great recipe on our site!).

Green Pesto Lentil Lasagna

FAN FAVORITE

Serves 4 — Prep: 15 minutes Cook: 1 hour 15 minutes Total: 1 hour 30 minutes

This is my go-to cozy dinner party dish. It looks impressive, tastes amazing, and is far simpler to make than a traditional lasagna, which might explain why it quickly became a fan favorite in our app. Lentils add the protein, mushrooms give it a meaty texture (and if mushrooms aren't your thing, zucchini or eggplant works just as well), and a good vegan pesto does most of the flavor heavy lifting.

LENTIL VEGGIE FILLING

1 tablespoon olive oil

1 medium shallot, chopped

12 ounces / 350g cremini mushrooms, thinly sliced

2 cups / 360g cooked brown lentils

2 cups / 60g fresh spinach, chopped

2 tablespoons Italian seasoning

½ teaspoon chile flakes

½ teaspoon fine sea salt

¼ teaspoon ground black pepper

BÉCHAMEL SAUCE

2 tablespoons unsalted vegan butter

¼ cup / 34g all-purpose flour

3 cups / 720ml unsweetened soy or almond milk

1 tablespoon nutritional yeast flakes

½ teaspoon fine sea salt

⅛ teaspoon ground nutmeg

Pinch of ground black pepper

ASSEMBLY

8 ounces / 225g dried lasagna sheets

¾ cup / 180g vegan green pesto

1½ cups / 180g shredded vegan cheese

Fresh basil (optional), for garnish

1. **MAKE THE LENTIL VEGGIE FILLING:** In a medium sauté pan, heat the oil over medium-high heat. Add the shallot and cook for 3 to 4 minutes, until lightly golden.

2. Add the mushrooms, lentils, spinach, Italian seasoning, chile flakes, salt, and pepper. Cook for 5 minutes, until the mushrooms soften. Set aside.

3. **MAKE THE BÉCHAMEL SAUCE:** In a medium saucepan, melt the butter over medium heat. Add the flour and cook, stirring constantly, for 2 to 3 minutes to toast the flour.

4. Slowly whisk in the milk in a thin, steady stream. Add the nutritional yeast, salt, nutmeg, and pepper. Simmer gently, whisking constantly, for 3 to 5 minutes, until the sauce has thickened enough to coat the back of a spoon.

5. **ASSEMBLE THE LASAGNA:** Preheat the oven to 375°F / 190°C.

6. Start with a thin layer of béchamel on the bottom of a 9-inch / 23cm square (or equivalent size) baking dish. Add a layer of lasagna sheets, then spread half of the mushroom mixture over the top.

7. Add more béchamel, a few spoonfuls of vegan pesto, and another layer of lasagna sheets. Repeat the layering until all the ingredients are used up. Finish with a generous layer of vegan cheese on top and a few dollops of pesto.

8. Bake, uncovered, for about 40 minutes, or until golden and bubbling.

9. Let cool slightly before serving. Top with fresh basil, if desired.

HEADS-UP: We used a store-bought pesto to keep things speedy, but if you're going the homemade route, I'd recommend our Basil Cashew Pesto (page 134).

Creamy Green Macaroni

Serves 4 — Prep: 15 minutes Cook: 25 minutes Total: 50 minutes

When I was in high school, I worked at a pasta restaurant and became utterly obsessed with creamy sauces. I mean, who doesn't love a rich, comforting pasta? While most of the dishes were delicious, they weren't exactly veggie-forward. This green macaroni is a more balanced take. It's packed with blended veggies and cashews for a creamy sauce that feels just as indulgent, but is a whole lot more nourishing. And if you're wondering whether to add the lemon zest and feta: yes. Always yes.

- ¾ cup / 100g raw cashews
- 12 ounces / 340g elbow macaroni or medium shell pasta
- ½ tablespoon vegetable oil
- 1 medium onion, chopped
- 1 medium zucchini, finely chopped
- ¾ cup / 105g frozen green peas
- 1½ cups / 45g fresh spinach
- ¾ cup / 12g fresh basil
- ¾ cup / 180ml unsweetened soy or almond milk
- 1½ tablespoons nutritional yeast flakes
- 2 garlic cloves
- ½ teaspoon fine sea salt
- ⅛ teaspoon chile flakes (optional)
- Grated zest and juice of ½ lemon
- ¼ cup / 34g unsalted roasted hazelnuts, chopped
- 2 ounces / 55g vegan feta, crumbled (about ⅓ cup)

1. The night before you plan to serve the macaroni, soak the cashews in plenty of water. The next day, drain them. If the cashews weren't soaked overnight, simply boil them in water for 10 minutes to soften.

2. Cook the pasta according to the package instructions. Drain and return it to the pot.

3. In a large pot, heat the oil over medium-high heat. Add the onion and cook for about 3 minutes, or until translucent. Add the zucchini and peas, and cook for 5 to 7 minutes, until the zucchini has softened. Transfer the mixture to a blender.

4. Add the soaked and drained cashews to the blender along with the spinach, basil, milk, nutritional yeast, garlic, salt, and chile flakes (if using). Blend until smooth.

5. Pour the sauce over the cooked pasta and toss to coat. Stir in the lemon juice.

6. Serve the pasta topped with lemon zest, chopped hazelnuts, and crumbled feta.

Lemony Tahini Tagliatelle

with Burst Cherry Tomatoes

Serves 4 — **Prep:** 10 minutes **Cook:** 35 minutes **Total:** 45 minutes

The star of this pasta is the tahini sauce: It's rich, nutty, and silky smooth. A good squeeze of lemon adds brightness; garlic makes it extra savory; and juicy, lightly burst tomatoes add just enough freshness to cut through all the creaminess. And while it might be tempting to skip the toasted bread crumbs, they do add a lovely bit of crunch at the end that's worth it.

- Fine sea salt
- 11 ounces / 300g tagliatelle
- 5 garlic cloves
- 1½ tablespoons vegetable oil
- ⅓ cup / 19g panko bread crumbs
- 1 large shallot, finely chopped
- 2 cups / 300g cherry tomatoes
- ½ cup / 130g tahini (see Heads-Up)
- 1 tablespoon extra-virgin olive oil
- Grated zest and juice of 1 lemon
- 1 tablespoon nutritional yeast flakes
- 1 teaspoon maple syrup
- 1 cup / 140g frozen green peas
- ½ cup / 8g fresh basil, thinly sliced

1. Bring a large pot of generously salted water to a boil. Add the tagliatelle and cook to al dente according to the package instructions. Reserving at least 1 cup / 240ml of pasta water (more if you'd like flexibility), drain the tagliatelle and set aside.

2. Crush 1 of the garlic cloves to a paste and mince the remaining 4 cloves.

3. In a large sauté pan, combine the crushed garlic, ½ tablespoon of the vegetable oil, the panko, and ⅛ teaspoon salt. Toast over medium-high heat for about 5 minutes, stirring often, until golden. Transfer to a plate.

4. In the now-empty pan, heat the remaining 1 tablespoon vegetable oil over medium-high heat. Add the shallot and minced garlic and cook for about 5 minutes, or until soft and golden.

5. Add the tomatoes and cook for another 7 to 8 minutes, until lightly burst.

6. Meanwhile, in a medium bowl, whisk together the tahini, olive oil, lemon zest, lemon juice, nutritional yeast, maple syrup, and 1 teaspoon fine sea salt. Slowly mix in the reserved pasta water to loosen the sauce. Start with 1 cup / 240ml and add more as needed, depending on how thick your tahini is.

7. Add the tahini sauce to the pan with the tomatoes, then add the cooked pasta and peas. Toss to coat. Cook for 3 minutes to warm the peas through.

8. Stir in the basil just before serving, and top with the toasted panko.

HEADS-UP: Tahini can vary a lot between brands, especially in how much the sesame seeds are roasted. Some are made from raw sesame seeds and taste pretty mild, while others are made from toasted seeds, which gives them a far richer, deeper flavor. That's the one you want here. The golden kind.

Baked Stuffed Pasta Shells

with Spinach & Tofu "Ricotta"

Serves 4 — Prep: 30 minutes Cook: 30 minutes Total: 1 hour

One of the things I love most about our recipe team is how often we bring inspiration back from our travels—not just ideas, but ingredients, too. When one teammate returned from Italy with a bag of jumbo pasta shells (and I mean JUMBO—far bigger than anything we can find at our local markets in the Netherlands), we knew exactly what we had to do: stuff them, of course! These shells are filled with a creamy, plant-based ricotta-style mixture and nestled into a rich, garlicky tomato sauce. Baked until golden and bubbling, it's a comforting dish that's both beautiful and delicious. Even if your shells are smaller than the ones we used, not to worry, the recipe still works beautifully.

- Fine sea salt
- 7 ounces / 200g jumbo shell pasta
- 1 tablespoon olive oil
- 4 garlic cloves, thinly sliced
- ¼ teaspoon chile flakes
- 2 cups / 500g jarred passata (or plain pasta sauce)
- ¼ cup / 4g fresh basil leaves, chopped
- 1½ cups / 170g frozen spinach, thawed
- 14 ounces / 395g firm tofu
- 1½ cups / 195g raw cashews
- ⅓ cup / 27g nutritional yeast flakes
- 1 tablespoon garlic powder
- ½ teaspoon freshly ground black pepper
- ⅛ teaspoon ground nutmeg
- ⅓ cup / 40g shredded vegan cheese of choice

1. Bring a large pot of generously salted water to a boil. Add the pasta shells and cook for 2 minutes less than the package instructions for al dente. Drain and set aside.

2. Meanwhile, in a small saucepan, warm the oil over medium-high heat. Add the garlic and chile flakes and cook, stirring, for 1 minute, until lightly golden.

3. Add the passata, basil, and ½ teaspoon fine sea salt. Reduce the heat to low and cook, uncovered, for about 7 minutes to thicken the sauce slightly. Transfer the sauce to a 9 × 13-inch / 23 × 33cm baking dish.

4. Position a rack in the upper third of the oven and preheat the oven to 425°F / 220°C.

5. Transfer the thawed spinach to a sieve set over a bowl and squeeze out any excess water. Reserve 3 tablespoons of the spinach water and set aside. (Save the remaining spinach water for soups or smoothies, if desired.)

6. In a food processor, blitz the tofu, cashews, nutritional yeast, garlic powder, pepper, nutmeg, 1 teaspoon fine sea salt, and the 3 tablespoons of reserved spinach water until smooth. Remove the blades, then mix in the squeezed spinach.

7. Fill the pasta shells with the tofu mixture, then arrange them over the sauce in the baking dish. Cover with the grated cheese.

8. Bake for about 15 minutes, until lightly golden. Serve warm.

One-Pot Creamy Mushroom Fusilli

FAN FAVORITE

Serves 4 — Prep: 10 minutes Cook: 20 minutes Total: 30 minutes

This mushroom pasta is the highest rated and most reviewed recipe from our website. I'm convinced its success comes down to two things: It's ridiculously simple and outrageously flavorful. Everything cooks in one pot, which I know for a lot of pasta-lovers is a big no-no, but this just works. And yes, coconut milk in pasta sounds a bit weird, but trust me, it works, too (and it doesn't taste overly coconutty). It reduces into a rich, velvety sauce, and the mushrooms cook down, taking on a savory, almost meaty texture. It's a total comfort dish that will likely earn a spot in your weekly rotation.

1 tablespoon olive oil

2 medium shallots, finely chopped

6 garlic cloves, minced

1 fresh red chile, seeded and minced

2½ cups / 600ml vegetable broth

1 (13.5-ounce / 400ml) can full-fat coconut milk

5 ounces / 140g button mushrooms, sliced

10 ounces / 285g oyster mushrooms, sliced

1 pound / 455g fusilli pasta

¼ cup / 38g sun-dried tomatoes in oil, drained and chopped

2 tablespoons nutritional yeast flakes

1 tablespoon reduced-sodium soy sauce

1 teaspoon sweet paprika

1 teaspoon fine sea salt

Pinch of freshly ground black pepper

4 cups / 120g fresh spinach

Fresh basil (optional), for serving

1. In a large pot, heat the oil over high heat. Add the shallots, garlic, and chile and sauté for about 3 minutes, until lightly golden.

2. Add the vegetable broth, coconut milk, both mushrooms, pasta, sun-dried tomatoes, nutritional yeast, soy sauce, paprika, salt, and pepper and bring to a boil. Reduce the heat to a gentle simmer, partially cover, and cook, stirring occasionally to prevent sticking, for about 15 minutes, or until the pasta is al dente.

3. Stir in the spinach and cook until wilted. Taste and add more salt and pepper if you like. If desired, finish with a sprinkle of basil.

Stir-Fries & Rice

Pineapple Tempeh Stir-Fry

Serves 2 or 3 — Prep: 15 minutes Cook: 20 minutes
Total: 35 minutes, plus 20 minutes marinating time

This sweet and spicy stir-fry is tossed with juicy pineapple (always a yes from me!) and finished with roasted cashews on top (optional but highly recommended) for extra crunch. It might just become your new favorite way to use tempeh. And a quick PSA: Freshness makes a BIG difference when it comes to tempeh. The newer it is, the milder and nuttier the taste, so if it smells overly sour, it might be past its prime. When in doubt, give it a quick sniff before using and try to buy it from a store with high turnover.

MARINATED TEMPEH

2 tablespoons soy sauce
2 tablespoons light brown sugar
2 tablespoons pineapple juice, reserved from the can
1 tablespoon sambal oelek
1 tablespoon toasted sesame oil
1 tablespoon rice vinegar
1 teaspoon grated fresh ginger
1 garlic clove, crushed to a paste
8 ounces / 225g tempeh

STIR-FRY

¾ cup / 180ml cold water
2 teaspoons cornstarch
1 tablespoon vegetable oil
1 red bell pepper, chopped
½ cup / 125g canned pineapple chunks, drained, chopped
1 green onion, cut into 1-inch / 2.5cm pieces
Cooked white or brown rice, for serving

OPTIONAL GARNISHES

Unsalted roasted cashews
Toasted sesame seeds
Fresh cilantro leaves

1. **MARINATE THE TEMPEH:** In a medium bowl, whisk together the soy sauce, brown sugar, pineapple juice, sambal, sesame oil, vinegar, ginger, and garlic. Crumble the tempeh into the bowl using your hands, breaking it into small, bite-size pieces. Stir to coat, then set aside to marinate for at least 20 minutes, or up to 8 hours.

2. **MAKE THE STIR-FRY:** In a small bowl, whisk together the cold water and cornstarch until smooth. (Cornstarch should always be mixed with cold water first, as it can clump if added directly to warm liquids.)

3. In a large sauté pan, heat the vegetable oil over medium-high heat. Add the marinated tempeh along with all the marinade and cook uncovered, stirring occasionally, for 6 to 7 minutes, until the tempeh is golden and most of the liquid has been absorbed.

4. Pour in the cornstarch mixture, then add the bell pepper, pineapple, and green onion. Reduce the heat to medium and cook for 4 to 5 minutes, until the sauce has thickened slightly and the bell pepper is tender to your liking.

5. Serve the sweet and tangy stir-fry over rice. Top with any or all of the garnishes.

Kalamata Olive & Cherry Tomato Risotto

Serves 4 — Prep: 10 minutes Cook: 35 minutes Total: 45 minutes

Back in the day, Nigella Lawson's cooking show was my ultimate comfort show. I'd curl up on the couch and lose myself in her buttery voice and effortless meals. In one episode, she called the act of stirring risotto meditative. Now, every time I make risotto, I think of her and that mindset shift. Risotto has this way of making the kitchen feel calm. It's not complicated, but it does ask you to be there with it, stirring mindfully. I love that it forces me to slow down. This version comes together with just a few simple Mediterranean ingredients and feels like a win at the end of the day.

6 cups / 1.4L vegetable broth

1 tablespoon vegetable oil

1 medium onion, finely chopped

½ teaspoon fine sea salt

2 tablespoons tomato paste

2 cups / 400g arborio rice

2 cups / 300g cherry tomatoes, halved

1 cup / 135g pitted kalamata olives, chopped

1 (15-ounce / 425g) can cannellini beans, drained and rinsed

¾ cup / 12g fresh basil, coarsely chopped

2 tablespoons nutritional yeast flakes

2 teaspoons white wine vinegar

⅛ teaspoon freshly ground black pepper

Roasted pine nuts (optional), for garnish

Vegan parmesan (optional), for garnish

1. Pour the broth into a medium saucepan and keep it warm over low heat on the stove.

2. In a large sauté pan, heat the oil over medium-high heat. Add the onion and salt and cook for about 4 minutes, or until lightly golden.

3. Reduce the heat to medium and stir in the tomato paste. Cook for 1 minute, stirring constantly to toast. Add the rice, tomatoes, and olives and cook, stirring often, for 2 minutes to toast the rice slightly.

4. Add about 1 cup / 240ml of the warm broth and let the rice simmer gently. Stir often until the liquid is fully absorbed. Continue adding the broth, about 1 cup / 240ml at a time, stirring until it is absorbed before adding more. Take your time with this step as it helps the rice become creamy and perfectly tender.

5. If the rice is still too firm after all the broth has been absorbed, add more broth as needed. Once the rice is al dente and creamy—this usually takes 25 to 30 minutes—stir in the beans, basil, nutritional yeast, vinegar, and black pepper. Taste and add more salt if you like.

6. Allow to heat through, then serve warm. Garnish as desired.

Tempeh Coconut Rice
with Peanut Sauce

Serves 3 to 4 — Prep: 15 minutes Cook: 25 minutes Total: 40 minutes

Trips to Indonesia to visit my husband's family always send me home with new cravings. This recipe isn't a traditional Indonesian dish, but it's inspired by many of the flavors we came to love while we were there, especially peanut butter–based sauces, which are spicy, tangy, and a little sweet (honestly, I'd happily drizzle this sauce on anything). It's served with sambal roasted tempeh and broccoli, with coconut rice as the perfect backdrop. Toasted coconut stirred in makes the rice fragrant and turns the whole meal into something special without much extra effort.

ROASTED TEMPEH & BROCCOLI

8 ounces / 225g tempeh
3 tablespoons vegetable oil
1 tablespoon sambal oelek
¼ teaspoon fine sea salt
1 medium broccoli, cut into florets

COCONUT RICE

1 cup / 200g long-grain white rice
1¼ cups / 300ml water
⅓ cup / 25g unsweetened shredded coconut, toasted

PEANUT SAUCE

½ cup / 130g natural peanut butter
¼ cup / 60ml water
Juice of 1 lime
1 garlic clove, crushed to a paste
2 tablespoons maple syrup
½ tablespoon sambal oelek
⅛ teaspoon fine sea salt

ASSEMBLY

8 ounces / 225g sugar snap peas
1 green onion (optional), sliced
¼ cup / 37g unsalted roasted peanuts (optional), chopped

1. Preheat the oven to 400°F / 200°C. Line a baking sheet with parchment paper.

2. **ROAST THE TEMPEH AND BROCCOLI:** Crumble the tempeh into small, bite-size pieces. The smaller the better. Transfer to a medium bowl and mix with 2 tablespoons of the oil, the sambal, and salt. Spread the seasoned tempeh over one-half of the baking sheet.

3. Toss the broccoli with the remaining 1 tablespoon oil and spread it on the other half of the baking sheet.

4. Roast for 20 minutes, or until the broccoli has slightly browned and the tempeh is golden.

5. **MEANWHILE, MAKE THE COCONUT RICE:** Rinse the rice. In a medium saucepan, combine the rice and water. Cover, bring to a gentle simmer, and cook over low heat until the water is absorbed, 12 to 15 minutes.

6. Once cooked, fluff the rice with a fork and gently mix in the toasted coconut. Keep covered until ready to serve.

7. **MAKE THE PEANUT SAUCE:** In a small bowl, whisk together the peanut butter, water, lime juice, garlic, maple syrup, sambal, and salt until smooth. The sauce may seem thin at first but will thicken as you stir. Add more water if you prefer a thinner consistency.

8. **ASSEMBLE:** Bring a medium pot of water to a boil. Add the snap peas and cook until bright green and just tender, about 2 minutes. Immediately drain and rinse under cold water to stop the cooking. Optionally, slice the snap peas in half lengthwise.

9. To serve, divide the coconut rice among bowls and top with the roasted tempeh, broccoli, and snap peas. Drizzle with the peanut sauce. If desired, garnish with green onions and peanuts.

Sticky Eggplant Tofu Stir-Fry

Serves 4 — Prep: 15 minutes Cook: 25 minutes
Total: 40 minutes, plus 15 minutes soaking time

I know a recipe is a keeper when our whole team keeps making it at home well after it's been tested in the studio. This is one of those favorites. Soaking the eggplant in salted water helps reduce bitterness and draw out excess moisture, so it roasts up beautifully tender and soaks up the sticky, savory sauce. Paired with tofu, it makes an easy weeknight meal that's every bit as good as takeout.

ROASTED EGGPLANT

2 medium eggplants (about 1½ pounds / 680g total)

1 teaspoon fine sea salt

2 tablespoons vegetable oil

FRIED TOFU

14 ounces / 395g firm tofu, pressed

2 tablespoons cornstarch

1 tablespoon vegetable oil

STIR-FRY SAUCE

2 garlic cloves, crushed to a paste

¼ cup / 60ml reduced-sodium soy sauce

¼ cup / 60ml water

2 tablespoons maple syrup

1 tablespoon rice vinegar

1 tablespoon sriracha

1 teaspoon toasted sesame oil

2 teaspoons cornstarch

ASSEMBLY

½ fresh red chile, minced

Cooked rice, for serving

Toasted sesame seeds (optional), for garnish

Sliced green onion (optional), for garnish

1. **ROAST THE EGGPLANT:** Cut the eggplant into 1-inch / 2.5cm pieces. Place the eggplant pieces in a large bowl and cover with enough water to fully submerge. Stir in the salt, then place a pot lid or plate on top to weight the eggplant down. Let soak for 15 minutes.

2. Preheat the oven to 425°F / 220°C. Line a baking sheet with parchment paper.

3. Drain the eggplant and pat dry with a clean kitchen towel. Transfer the eggplant to the prepared baking sheet and toss with the oil.

4. Bake for 20 to 25 minutes, stirring halfway through, until golden and tender.

5. **FRY THE TOFU:** Cut the tofu into ½ inch / 1cm cubes. In a medium bowl, toss the tofu with the cornstarch until evenly coated. In a large sauté pan, heat the oil over medium-high heat. Cook the tofu for about 8 minutes, or until golden on all sides.

6. **MAKE THE STIR-FRY SAUCE:** In a small bowl, whisk together the garlic, soy sauce, water, maple syrup, vinegar, sriracha, sesame oil, and cornstarch.

7. Transfer the cooked tofu to a bowl. To the now-empty sauté pan, pour in the stir-fry sauce and cook over medium heat for 2 to 3 minutes, until slightly thickened.

8. **ASSEMBLE THE STIR-FRY:** Add the roasted eggplant and cooked tofu to the pan. Stir to coat evenly in the sauce. Stir in the minced chile.

9. Serve the sticky eggplant and tofu mixture over rice. If desired, garnish with sesame seeds and green onions.

HEADS-UP: The stir-fry sauce is worth bookmarking. It works beautifully with any combination of vegetables and proteins, even outside this recipe.

Korean-Style "Ground Beef" Bowls

Serves 4 —— Prep: 15 minutes Cook: 20 minutes Total: 35 minutes

My husband and I have made this for dinner more times than I can count. It's inspired by Korean bulgogi, known for its savory, caramelized flavors, but in this version we swap the meat for vegan ground beef. The sauce that coats the "beef" is the best part, and over the years I've taken a few liberties with it. Traditionally, bulgogi includes grated pear, but I usually have apples on hand, so I started using those instead. Eventually, to keep things simple, I switched to applesauce. Honestly, any of them will do. Serve it over rice, pile on some quick cooked veggies, and whatever you do, don't skip the kimchi. The sour, tangy crunch is essential (at least for me).

1 tablespoon vegetable oil

1 pound / 455g vegan ground beef, such as Beyond Meat or Impossible

¼ small onion, thinly sliced

⅓ cup / 80g unsweetened applesauce, or ½ pear or red apple, grated

4 garlic cloves, minced

3 tablespoons reduced-sodium soy sauce

2 tablespoons light brown sugar

1½ tablespoons toasted sesame oil

1½ tablespoons rice vinegar

1 tablespoon toasted sesame seeds

⅛ teaspoon ground black pepper

2 carrots, thinly sliced

7 ounces / 200g broccolini

¼ teaspoon fine sea salt

Cooked short- or medium-grain white rice, for serving

¾ cup / 115g vegan kimchi

OPTIONAL GARNISHES

Toasted sesame seeds

Sliced green onion

Sliced small radishes

1. In a large skillet, heat ½ tablespoon of the vegetable oil over medium-high heat. Add the vegan ground beef and use a spatula to break it into smaller pieces. Cook for about 6 minutes, or until browned.

2. In a small bowl, stir together the onion, applesauce, garlic, soy sauce, brown sugar, sesame oil, vinegar, sesame seeds, and pepper.

3. Add the sauce to the browned beef in the pan and cook, stirring occasionally, for 5 to 8 minutes, until glossy and slightly reduced.

4. In a separate large sauté pan, heat the remaining ½ tablespoon vegetable oil over medium heat. Add the carrots, broccolini, and salt. Cook for 5 minutes, or until just tender to your liking. If needed, add a splash of water to the pan to help the veggies steam.

5. Serve the vegan ground beef with cooked rice, veggies, and kimchi. Top with any or all of the garnishes.

Coconut Biryani
with Pan-Fried Spiced Tofu

Serves 4 — Prep: 20 minutes Cook: 1 hour Total: 1 hour 20 minutes

Biryani is one of the most iconic rice dishes from the Indian subcontinent, known for its bold spices, rich layers, and the kind of slow cooking that fills the whole house with mouthwatering aromas. Traditionally, it's made with marinated meat or vegetables, saffron-infused rice, and a long list of spices. This version keeps the essence but simplifies the steps: fewer spices, a golden turmeric milk instead of saffron, and the same classic layering—only with caramelized onions, raisins, and cashews for a naturally sweet and fragrant base. For a hearty plant-based finish, it is topped with golden pan-fried tofu.

1 cup / 200g basmati rice, rinsed
4 cups / 960ml water
2 bay leaves
1 cinnamon stick
3 tablespoons vegetable oil
2 medium onions, thinly sliced
1½ teaspoons fine sea salt
1 carrot, finely chopped
⅓ cup / 31g unsweetened shredded coconut
¼ cup / 33g raw cashews
2 tablespoons raisins
2 tablespoons garam masala
½ cup / 120ml unsweetened soy or almond milk
½ teaspoon ground turmeric
14 ounces / 395g firm tofu, torn into ½-inch / 1cm chunks
½ teaspoon onion powder
Unsweetened coconut yogurt (optional), for serving

1. In a medium pot, combine the rice, water, bay leaves, and cinnamon stick. Bring to a simmer and cook for 5 minutes. Drain and set aside. Discard the bay leaves and cinnamon.

2. In a large sauté pan, heat 2 tablespoons of the oil over medium heat. Add the onions and ½ teaspoon of the salt. Cook for 20 to 25 minutes, until golden and caramelized. Add splashes of water as needed to deglaze the pan. Remove half of the onions and set them aside for later.

3. To the onions remaining in the pan, add the carrot, coconut, cashews, raisins, and 1½ tablespoons of the garam masala. Cook for 3 minutes, allowing the flavors to meld.

4. Spread the cooked rice evenly on top of the vegetable mixture, followed by the reserved caramelized onions.

5. In a small bowl, mix the milk with the turmeric and ½ teaspoon of the salt. Pour the turmeric milk over the rice, then cover and cook over low heat without stirring for 10 to 13 minutes.

6. In a large skillet, heat the remaining 1 tablespoon oil over medium-high heat. Add the tofu along with the onion powder, remaining ½ tablespoon garam masala, and remaining ½ teaspoon salt. Cook, stirring occasionally, for about 8 minutes, or until golden on all sides.

7. Once the rice is cooked, gently mix everything together. Serve warm with the tofu on top and yogurt (if using) on the side.

Mujadara with Garlicky Tahini & Salata

Serves 4 — Prep: 15 minutes Cook: 40 minutes Total: 55 minutes

This comforting Middle Eastern dish gets its depth from slow-caramelized onions and warm spices. For a weeknight shortcut, I use canned lentils instead of cooking them from dry, then serve it with a crisp salata and a generous swirl of garlicky tahini.

CARAMELIZED ONIONS

2 medium onions, thinly sliced

2 tablespoons olive oil

½ teaspoon fine sea salt

MUJADARA

1¼ cups / 250g basmati rice

1 tablespoon olive oil

½ tablespoon ground cumin

1 teaspoon ground coriander

1 teaspoon dried mint leaves

1 teaspoon fine sea salt

¼ teaspoon ground black pepper

1¾ cups / 420ml water

2 (15-ounce / 425g) cans brown lentils, drained and rinsed

TAHINI SAUCE

⅓ cup / 85g tahini

Juice of ½ lemon

1 garlic clove, crushed to a paste

3 tablespoons water

½ tablespoon agave syrup

⅛ teaspoon fine sea salt

TOMATO-CUCUMBER SALATA

2 medium tomatoes, chopped

½ English cucumber, chopped

Juice of ½ lemon

¼ teaspoon dried mint leaves

¼ teaspoon fine sea salt

1. **MAKE THE CARAMELIZED ONIONS:** Take one or two of the onion slices, finely chop, and set aside for the tomato-cucumber salata.

2. In a large skillet, heat the oil over medium heat. Add the remaining sliced onions and salt. Cook, stirring occasionally, for 25 to 30 minutes, until deeply caramelized. If necessary, deglaze the pan with splashes of water.

3. **MAKE THE MUJADARA:** Rinse the rice until the water runs mostly clear, then drain well. In a large sauté pan, heat the oil over medium heat. Add the rice, cumin, coriander, dried mint, salt, and pepper and toast, stirring constantly, for 1 to 2 minutes.

4. Pour in the water, cover, and bring to a boil. Reduce to a gentle simmer and cook for 12 to 15 minutes, until the rice is tender.

5. Gently stir the lentils and one-third of the caramelized onions into the rice. Cover with a lid again and let the rice rest off the heat for 5 minutes.

6. **MAKE THE TAHINI SAUCE:** In a small bowl, combine the tahini, lemon juice, garlic, water, agave, and salt.

7. **MAKE THE SALATA:** In a small bowl, combine the reserved finely chopped onion, tomatoes, cucumber, lemon juice, dried mint, and salt.

8. Serve the mujadara topped with the remaining caramelized onions alongside the salata and a dollop of the tahini sauce. If desired, serve with toasted flatbread.

Golden Rice
with Za'atar-Roasted Chickpeas & Broccoli

Serves 3 —— Prep: 10 minutes Cook: 25 minutes Total: 35 minutes

This is a meal that feels both nourishing and easy to pull together. While the broccoli and chickpeas roast in the oven, the spiced golden rice gently simmers on the stove, filling the kitchen with the warm scent of cumin and turmeric. For maximum efficiency, I like to use that time to whisk together a quick sauce featuring two ingredients I'm pretty obsessed with: tahini and dill. It all comes together with minimal effort, making it perfect for busy weeknights or easy meal prep.

1 medium broccoli, cut into florets

1 (15-ounce / 425g) can chickpeas, drained and rinsed

2 tablespoons olive oil

2 tablespoons za'atar spice mix

Fine sea salt

1 cup / 200g long-grain white rice, rinsed

1¼ cups / 300ml plus 3 tablespoons water

¾ teaspoon ground cumin

½ teaspoon ground turmeric

Pinch of freshly ground black pepper

⅓ cup / 85g tahini (see Heads-Up)

Juice of 1 lemon

1 garlic clove, crushed to a paste

3 tablespoons fresh dill, finely chopped

1 tablespoon agave or maple syrup

½ cup / 100g pickled red onions

1. Preheat the oven to 400°F / 200°C. Line a baking sheet with parchment paper.

2. Place the broccoli and chickpeas on the prepared baking sheet, drizzle with the oil, za'atar, and ½ teaspoon salt. Toss to coat.

3. Roast for 18 to 22 minutes, until lightly browned.

4. In a medium saucepan, combine the rice, 1¼ cups / 300ml of the water, the cumin, turmeric, pepper, and ½ teaspoon salt. Cover and bring to a boil. Reduce to a gentle simmer and cook for 12 to 15 minutes, until the water is absorbed. Let sit, covered, for 5 minutes before fluffing.

5. In a small bowl, combine the tahini, lemon juice, garlic, dill, agave, the remaining 3 tablespoons water, and ⅛ teaspoon salt. Mix until smooth. The mixture might look thin at first, but keep mixing, it will continue to thicken. Taste and add more salt if you like.

6. Serve the golden rice topped with roasted broccoli and chickpeas, garnished with pickled onion, and finished with a drizzle of tahini-dill sauce.

HEADS-UP: As always, I recommend golden tahini made from roasted sesame seeds, as its deeper, nuttier flavor really elevates the sauce compared to the paler kind made from raw seeds.

Spicy Tofu Sushi Bake

Serves 4 — Prep: 20 minutes Cook: 25 minutes Total: 45 minutes

I adore sushi, but I don't always have the patience to let the rice cool or to roll and slice everything neatly. Enter the sushi bake. The tofu is shredded and mixed with crushed nori to give it a savory, sea-like flavor, then layered over seasoned rice and baked until warm and golden. Right before serving, I like to top it with creamy avocado, crisp cucumbers, and a generous drizzle of sriracha and mayo. Scoop it all up with snacking seaweed, and just like that, an unassuming weeknight turns into a plant-based sushi feast.

- 1½ cups / 300g short-grain white rice
- 2 cups / 480ml water
- 2 tablespoons rice vinegar
- ½ tablespoon sugar
- ½ teaspoon fine sea salt
- 14 ounces / 395g firm tofu, pressed (see How to Press Tofu, page 37)
- 2 nori seaweed sheets
- ¼ cup / 60g plus 2 tablespoons vegan mayonnaise
- 3 tablespoons sriracha
- 1½ tablespoons reduced-sodium soy sauce
- ½ tablespoon onion powder
- 1 avocado, sliced
- ½ English cucumber, sliced
- 4 (0.17-ounce / 5g) packages roasted seaweed snacks
- Toasted sesame seeds (optional), for garnish
- Sliced green onions (optional), for garnish

1. Rinse the rice in a fine-mesh sieve under cold water until the water runs clear. In a medium saucepan, combine the rice and water. Cover and simmer gently for 12 to 15 minutes, until the rice is tender and all the water is absorbed.

2. In a small bowl, whisk together the vinegar, sugar, and salt until dissolved.

3. Transfer the cooked rice to a 9-inch / 23cm square (or equivalent size) baking dish. Pour the vinegar mixture over the rice and gently fold it in.

4. Preheat the oven to 400°F / 200°C.

5. Using the large holes of a box grater, grate the tofu into a large bowl.

6. Tear the nori sheets into small pieces and place them in a spice grinder. Blitz until finely ground. (Alternatively, use a sharp knife or scissors to chop the nori very finely.)

7. Add the nori to the grated tofu, then add ¼ cup / 60g of the mayo, 1 tablespoon of the sriracha, the soy sauce, and onion powder. Gently mix until evenly coated. Spread the tofu mixture evenly over the rice.

8. Bake for 10 to 15 minutes, until the top is lightly golden.

9. Allow to cool slightly before drizzling with the remaining 2 tablespoons each of sriracha and mayo.

10. Serve with avocado and cucumber slices, and crispy snacking seaweed for scooping. If desired, garnish with sesame seeds and sliced green onions.

Curries & Stews

Simple Vegan "Butter Chicken"

FAN FAVORITE

Serves 4 — Prep: 15 minutes Cook: 20 minutes Total: 35 minutes

If there's one dish I always make when nonvegan friends come to visit, it's this. Flag it, bookmark it, come back to it—it's a crowd-pleaser through and through. In fact, it's one of the most popular recipes on our entire site. Butter chicken is a classic, and this plant-based version delivers all the comfort and richness of the original.

Traditionally, the chicken is marinated in a spiced yogurt mixture to tenderize and build flavor. In our original recipe on the blog, we did the same with tofu—coating it in yogurt and baking it to mimic that texture. But after making this recipe for years (I could make it with my eyes closed), I've simplified the process even more. These days, I pan-fry the tofu and stir the spices and yogurt directly into the curry. It's just as delicious, but quicker, easier, and more weeknight-friendly.

- **2 tablespoons vegetable oil**
- **14 ounces / 395g firm tofu,** pressed (see How to Press Tofu, page 37), cut into ¾-inch / 2cm cubes
- **1½ teaspoons fine sea salt**
- **1 large onion,** chopped
- **5 garlic cloves,** minced
- **1 fresh red chile,** seeded and minced
- **2 teaspoons grated fresh ginger**
- **1½ tablespoons garam masala**
- **1½ tablespoons ground coriander**
- **1½ tablespoons ground cumin**
- **½ teaspoon ground turmeric**
- **1 (14.5-ounce / 410g) can diced tomatoes**
- **1 (13.5-ounce / 400ml) can full-fat coconut milk**
- **¼ cup / 65g tomato paste**
- **½ tablespoon agave syrup**
- **½ cup / 130g unsweetened soy or almond yogurt**
- **4 Vegan Garlic Naan (page 174),** for serving
- **Cooked rice,** for serving

1. In a large skillet, heat 1 tablespoon of the oil over medium-high heat. Add the tofu and ½ teaspoon of the salt and cook for about 8 minutes, until golden on most sides.

2. In a large sauté pan, heat the remaining 1 tablespoon oil over medium-high heat. Add the onion, garlic, chile, and ginger and cook for 4 minutes, or until lightly golden.

3. Stir in the garam masala, coriander, cumin, turmeric, and the remaining 1 teaspoon salt. Stirring constantly, toast the spices for 1 minute. Add the tomatoes, coconut milk, tomato paste, and agave and bring to a gentle simmer.

4. Optionally, use an immersion blender to blend until partially smooth, leaving a bit of texture. (Alternatively, transfer about half of the mixture to a countertop blender and puree until smooth, then return it to the pot.)

5. Stir in the yogurt, then add the fried tofu and let heat through.

6. Serve with naan and cooked rice.

Eggplant Lentil Stew
with Hummus & Pita

Serves 4 — Prep: 15 minutes Cook: 35 minutes Total: 50 minutes

I adore the combo of eggplant and tomatoes, and this is a simple dinner I make when I want something wholesome but don't want to spend too much time in the kitchen. The eggplant turns soft and buttery, the tomatoes add juiciness, and the pomegranate molasses gives it a little sweet and tangy kick. Add some lentils for extra substance and protein, and you've got a meal that's comforting but still light. I like to spoon it over a generous layer of hummus and scoop it all up with a warm toasted pita.

- **3 medium eggplants (12 lbs / 905g total),** cut into 2-inch / 5cm pieces
- **2 tablespoons olive oil**
- **1 teaspoon fine sea salt**
- **1 large onion,** finely chopped
- **4 garlic cloves,** minced
- **2 fresh red chiles,** seeded and minced
- **3 tablespoons tomato paste**
- **1 (15-ounce / 425g) can brown lentils,** drained and rinsed
- **3 medium tomatoes,** chopped
- **3 tablespoons pomegranate molasses**
- **¼ teaspoon freshly ground black pepper**
- **1⅓ cups / 330g hummus**
- **2 tablespoons fresh mint leaves,** thinly sliced, for garnish
- **4 small pita breads,** toasted, for serving

1. Preheat the oven to 425°F / 220°C. Line a baking sheet with parchment paper.

2. Place the eggplants on the prepared baking sheet and drizzle with 1 tablespoon of the oil and ¼ teaspoon of the salt. Toss to coat.

3. Roast for about 25 minutes, stirring once halfway through, until the eggplant is soft.

4. In a large sauté pan, heat the remaining 1 tablespoon oil over medium-high heat. Add the onion, garlic, and chiles and cook for 4 minutes, or until the onion is lightly golden.

5. Add the tomato paste and cook, stirring constantly, for 1 minute to toast it slightly. Stir in the roasted eggplant, lentils, tomatoes, pomegranate molasses, pepper, and remaining ¾ teaspoon salt. Cook for 5 to 7 minutes, until the tomatoes have softened and everything is heated through.

6. Spread a generous layer of hummus on each serving plate. Spoon the lentil and eggplant stew over top, garnish with mint, and serve with warm pita on the side.

Vegan Persian Fesenjān

Serves 4 — Prep: 20 minutes Cook: 35 minutes Total: 55 minutes

This dish brings back so many memories from when I was little. It's called fesenjān, or fesenjoon, and it's an Iranian dish my mom would make all the time. I'll be honest, though, as a kid, I wasn't the biggest fan. The flavors felt too bold and complicated for me to fully enjoy. But now it's one of the dishes I genuinely look forward to most when I visit home. The sauce is rich and comforting, made with walnuts and pomegranate molasses, and it has this sweet and tangy balance that's just so unique. Traditionally it's made with chicken or duck, but in this plant-based version we're using seitan instead. Its meaty texture holds up beautifully in the velvety sauce.

10 saffron threads
1¾ cups / 155g raw walnuts
1 tablespoon vegetable oil
1 medium onion, chopped
¼ cup / 65g tomato paste
½ teaspoon ground turmeric
Pinch of ground cinnamon
Pinch of fine sea salt
Pinch of freshly ground black pepper
2 cups / 480ml vegetable broth
8 ounces / 225g seitan, torn into bite-size chunks
2 tablespoons pomegranate molasses
Cooked basmati rice (see Heads-Up), for serving
Fresh cilantro (optional), for garnish
Pomegranate seeds (optional), for garnish

1. Bloom the saffron by sprinkling it over an ice cube set in a small bowl and letting it melt completely.

2. In a food processor, grind the walnuts until finely ground.

3. In a medium sauté pan, heat the oil over medium-high heat. Add the onion and cook for about 4 minutes, or until lightly golden.

4. Add the ground walnuts and toast, stirring often, for 2 to 3 minutes.

5. Stir in the tomato paste, turmeric, cinnamon, salt, and pepper and cook for 1 to 2 minutes to allow the spices to toast and become fragrant.

6. Pour in the saffron and its liquid, along with the vegetable broth, seitan, and pomegranate molasses. Cover, reduce the heat to medium-low, and simmer gently, stirring occasionally, for 20 minutes to let the flavors develop.

7. Serve the fesenjān alongside warm rice. If desired, garnish with cilantro and pomegranate seeds.

HEADS-UP: Optionally, to tint part of the rice yellow, grind a small pinch of saffron threads and steep in hot water for 5 to 10 minutes. When the rice is cooked, mix the saffron liquid with a small portion of the rice to color it yellow. Use it as a garnish or mix it back into the rest of the rice.

Three-Bean Chili

Serves 4 — Prep: 15 minutes Cook: 45 minutes Total: 1 hour

This one-pot chili is a staple in our home. It's protein-packed with three types of beans, though any beans you have on hand will do. What makes it unique is a small handful of walnuts (optional, but worth it) that adds bite and richness and makes it feel extra hearty. I almost always make a big batch since it freezes beautifully, so future me has something warm and comforting ready to enjoy.

2 tablespoons vegetable oil

1 large onion, finely chopped

4 garlic cloves, minced

2 carrots, very finely chopped

⅓ cup / 29g raw walnuts (optional), finely chopped

¼ cup / 33g Mexican seasoning or taco seasoning

3 tablespoons tomato paste

3 tablespoons minced canned chipotle peppers in adobo sauce

2 vegetable bouillon cubes

1 (28-ounce / 795g) can crushed tomatoes

1 (15-ounce / 425g) can kidney beans, drained and rinsed

1 (15-ounce / 425g) can pinto beans, drained and rinsed

1 (15-ounce / 425g) can black beans, drained and rinsed

1 tablespoon light brown sugar

½ tablespoon dried oregano

OPTIONAL GO-WITHS

Fresh cilantro

Vegan sour cream or yogurt

Sliced fresh or pickled jalapeño

Tortilla chips

1. In a large pot, heat the oil over medium-high heat. Add the onion and cook, stirring occasionally, for about 7 minutes, or until golden. Add splashes of water as needed to deglaze the pot.

2. Add the garlic, carrots, and walnuts (if using). Cover and cook, stirring often, for about 7 minutes, or until the carrots begin to soften slightly. Continue deglazing with splashes of water as needed.

3. Add the Mexican seasoning, tomato paste, and chipotle peppers and cook, stirring constantly, for 1 to 2 minutes to lightly toast the spices and paste.

4. Crumble the bouillon into the pot, then add the crushed tomatoes, kidney beans, pinto beans, black beans, brown sugar, and oregano. Bring to a boil. Reduce the heat to medium, cover, and simmer gently for about 25 minutes, until the carrots are soft and cooked to your liking. Stir occasionally.

5. Serve in bowls and with your desired toppings and accompaniments.

Satay Curry

Serves 4 —— **Prep:** 20 minutes **Cook:** 35 minutes **Total:** 55 minutes

This is what I make when I want a comforting and hearty meal. It's unapologetically rich and by no means light, perfect for a I-want-to-feel-fully-satisfied-and-curl-up-on-the-couch-afterward kind of meal. Inspired by the bold flavors of Indonesian cuisine, the tofu is nestled in a peanut coconut sauce that's creamy, savory, and a little spicy. I usually serve it with jasmine rice, which is a bit sticky, so it holds its shape beautifully for little "igloos of rice," as my husband, Robin, likes to call them. Just pack the rice into a small bowl, flip it onto the plate, and lift the bowl away for an easy yet elevated presentation.

- 1½ tablespoons vegetable oil
- 1 large onion, chopped
- 4 garlic cloves, minced
- 2 fresh red chiles, seeded and minced
- 1 red bell pepper, chopped
- 1 carrot, thinly sliced
- 1 (13.5-ounce / 400ml) can full-fat coconut milk
- 1 cup / 240ml vegetable broth
- ½ cup / 130g natural peanut butter
- 3 tablespoons reduced-sodium soy sauce
- 1 tablespoon light brown sugar
- 14 ounces / 395g firm tofu, pressed (see How to Press Tofu, page 37)
- ½ teaspoon ground coriander
- ½ teaspoon ground cumin
- ¼ teaspoon fine sea salt
- Juice of 1 lime

FOR SERVING

- Cooked jasmine rice
- Fresh cilantro (optional), for garnish
- Chopped roasted peanuts (optional), for garnish

1. In a large sauté pan, heat ½ tablespoon of the oil over medium-high heat. Add the onion, garlic, and chile and cook for about 5 minutes, or until lightly golden.

2. Stir in the bell pepper, carrot, coconut milk, broth, peanut butter, soy sauce, and brown sugar. Simmer for 12 to 15 minutes, until the vegetables are tender to your liking.

3. Meanwhile, tear the tofu into bite-size chunks and place them in a large bowl. Add the coriander, cumin, and salt and toss to coat.

4. In a large skillet, heat the remaining 1 tablespoon oil over medium-high heat. Add the tofu and cook for about 8 minutes, or until golden.

5. Add the tofu and lime juice to the vegetables and stir to heat through. Taste and add more salt if you like.

6. TO SERVE: Serve the curry with warm rice. If desired, garnish with cilantro and peanuts.

HEADS-UP: I personally prefer the soft bite of tofu, but we've tested this recipe with tempeh in place of tofu and it works well, too.

Super Green Butter Beans

FAN FAVORITE

Serves 2 or 3 —— Prep: 10 minutes Cook: 10 minutes Total: 20 minutes

This quickly became one of the most-loved recipes in our app. If you're low on energy and time but still want something nourishing, this is the recipe to turn to. Every time I make it, I think, "Why don't I make this more often?"

It's a vibrant, feel-good stew that's packed with greens, but thanks to plenty of fresh basil and a squeeze of lemon, it tastes bright and herby—not overly earthy. Butter beans (also known as lima beans) live up to their name, adding a rich, buttery texture and a healthy dose of plant protein. And don't skip the crunchy bread on the side. You'll want to use it to scoop up every last bite!

2 tablespoons vegetable oil
1 medium onion, diced
3 garlic cloves, minced
⅛ teaspoon fine sea salt
7 cups / 210g fresh spinach
Grated zest and juice ½ lemon
1 vegetable bouillon cube
½ cup / 120ml water
½ cup / 130g unsweetened soy or almond yogurt, plus more for serving
1 cup / 16g fresh basil leaves
1½ tablespoons nutritional yeast flakes
¼ teaspoon freshly ground black pepper
2 (15-ounce / 425g) cans lima beans (butter beans), drained and rinsed
½ tablespoon extra-virgin olive oil
¼ teaspoon chile flakes
Large slices whole-grain bread, toasted, for serving

1. In a large pot, heat the vegetable oil over medium-high heat. Add the onion, garlic, and salt and cook for 5 minutes, or until golden.

2. Add the spinach and cook for 1 to 2 minutes, until wilted. Transfer to a blender.

3. Add the lemon juice to the blender along with the bouillon cube, water, yogurt, basil, nutritional yeast, and pepper. Blend until smooth, then transfer back to the pot.

4. Add the butter beans to the pot and cook until everything is heated through.

5. Transfer to a serving bowl and garnish with the lemon zest, a dollop of yogurt, a drizzle of the olive oil, and the chile flakes. Serve with toasted bread.

One-Pot Creamy Tomato Chickpea Curry

Serves 4 — **Prep:** 15 minutes **Cook:** 15 minutes **Total:** 30 minutes

I know I've struck gold with a new recipe when my husband, Robin, asks for it three times in one week. The recipe is absurdly simple, comes together quickly with mostly pantry staples, but still delivers BIG on flavor. The whole seeds are my favorite part. They sizzle in the oil, fill the kitchen with the most amazing aroma, and add little bursts of flavor in every spoonful. It's creamy, comforting, and has been on repeat in our kitchen ever since I first made it.

1 tablespoon vegetable oil
2 teaspoons coriander seeds
2 teaspoons brown mustard seeds
1 large onion, finely chopped
6 garlic cloves, minced
2 tablespoons tomato paste
2 teaspoons grated fresh ginger
½ tablespoon fine sea salt
½ tablespoon curry powder
1 teaspoon ground cumin
½ teaspoon chile flakes
1 (13.5-ounce / 400ml) can full-fat coconut milk
1 (14.5-ounce / 410g) can diced tomatoes
1 (15-ounce / 425g) can chickpeas, drained and rinsed
2 cups / 60g fresh spinach, chopped
2 tablespoons tahini (optional)
Cooked brown rice or Vegan Garlic Naan (page 174), for serving

OPTIONAL GARNISHES

Fresh cilantro
Lime wedges
Sliced red onion

1. In a large pot, heat the oil over medium heat. Add the coriander and mustard seeds and cook, stirring, for about 1 minute, or until the mustard seeds start to pop.

2. Add the onion, raise the heat to medium-high, and cook for about 3 minutes, or until translucent.

3. Add the garlic and cook for 3 minutes, or until golden.

4. Add the tomato paste, ginger, salt, curry powder, cumin, and chile flakes. Stir to toast until fragrant, about 30 seconds.

5. Stir in the coconut milk, tomatoes, and chickpeas and cook for 5 minutes, uncovered, for the curry to thicken slightly.

6. Stir in the spinach and tahini (if using) and cook for about 2 minutes, or until the spinach has wilted.

7. Serve in bowls with warm rice or naan. Serve with any or all of the garnishes.

Spicy Miso Harissa Beans
with Toast

Serves 2 Prep: 10 minutes Cook: 15 minutes Total: 25 minutes

This is another quick, protein-packed, cook-it-all-in-one-pot-and-call-it-a-day kind of meal. It requires minimal effort and is really intensely flavored. The combination of spicy harissa and umami-rich miso might sound like an unusual pairing at first, but it just works. I love it with butter beans, but chickpeas or white beans are just as great. And, it's the kind of dish you can enjoy for any meal of the day: as a savory breakfast (think beans on toast), or for an uber-simple lunch or dinner.

½ tablespoon vegetable oil
1 medium shallot, finely chopped
¾ cup / 180ml cold water
1 tablespoon cornstarch
1 vegetable bouillon cube, crumbled
1½ tablespoons harissa paste, or less for less spicy
1½ tablespoons nutritional yeast flakes
1 tablespoon white miso paste
1 tablespoon rice vinegar
2 (15-ounce / 425g) cans lima beans (butter beans), drained and rinsed
½ cup / 8g fresh parsley, finely chopped
Freshly ground black pepper
4 large slices whole-grain bread, toasted
Lemon wedges (optional), for serving

1. In a medium sauté pan, heat the oil over medium-high heat. Add the shallot and cook for about 3 minutes, or until golden.

2. In a small bowl, whisk together the water and cornstarch until smooth.

3. Pour the cornstarch mixture into the pan along with the bouillon, harissa, nutritional yeast, miso, and vinegar. Cook for 2 to 3 minutes at a gentle simmer for the mixture to thicken.

4. Add the beans, parsley, and pepper to taste and cook for 3 to 5 minutes, until slightly thickened and heated through.

5. Serve the toast alongside the stew in a bowl. If desired, squeeze a lemon wedge over everything.

HEADS-UP: This dish is quite bold. If you'd like to mellow out the flavors or add a bit of creaminess, try stirring in a spoonful or two of tahini or yogurt.

Shahi Tofu Curry

Serves 4 — Prep: 15 minutes Cook: 25 minutes Total: 40 minutes

Indian cuisine has so many classics, from butter chicken to tikka masala to palak paneer. In my opinion, shahi curry, though less well-known, deserves a place among them. *Shahi* translates to "royal" in Hindi, and true to its name, this curry is fit for kings and queens. The sauce is made from cashews, tomatoes, and aromatic spices blended into a smooth paste and then combined with coconut milk for an extra layer of creamy indulgence.

2 tablespoons plus 2 teaspoons vegetable oil

2 medium tomatoes, chopped

1 medium onion, chopped

2 garlic cloves, minced

1 tablespoon grated fresh ginger

¼ cup / 33g raw cashews

4 whole cloves

3 cardamom pods, cracked

1 cinnamon stick

1 fresh green chile, such as Indian, Thai, or serrano, halved lengthwise

2 teaspoons cumin seeds

1 tablespoon garam masala

1 teaspoon ground turmeric

¾ teaspoon fine sea salt

1 (13.5-ounce / 400ml) can full-fat coconut milk

14 ounces / 395g firm tofu, cut into triangles ¼ inch / 5mm thick

10 saffron threads

Cooked rice or Vegan Garlic Naan (page 174), for serving

Fresh cilantro (optional), for garnish

1. In a large pot, heat 2 tablespoons of the oil over medium-high heat. Add the tomatoes, onion, garlic, ginger, and cashews and cook for 10 minutes, or until the tomatoes soften.

2. Transfer the cooked mixture to a small food processor and blend until smooth.

3. Return the now-empty pot to medium heat and warm the remaining 2 teaspoons oil. Add the whole cloves, cardamom pods, cinnamon stick, green chile, and cumin seeds and toast for about 2 minutes, or until the spices start to pop.

4. Add the blended mixture to the pot, along with the garam masala, turmeric, salt, and coconut milk. Let everything heat through.

5. Add the tofu and saffron and gently stir to heat through. Remove the cinnamon stick, whole cloves, cardamom pods, and green chile from the curry. Taste and add more salt, if desired.

6. Serve the curry alongside the warm rice or naan and garnish as desired.

Desserts

Gluten-Free Tahini Chocolate Chip Cookies

Makes 8 cookies — Prep: 15 minutes Cook: 30 minutes Total: 45 minutes

You could probably make this right now without even going to the store. That's what I love most about these cookies: just a few simple pantry staples coming together to make something that tastes like it's straight from a bakery. Most gluten-free cookies call for specialty flours that can be tricky to find, but this one skips flour altogether. How cool is that?

1 cup / 255g tahini (see Heads-Up)

½ cup / 120ml maple syrup

1 tablespoon cornstarch

½ teaspoon baking soda

½ teaspoon pure vanilla extract

2.3 ounces / 65g dairy-free dark chocolate (50% to 60% cacao), chopped, plus more (optional) for topping

2 teaspoons toasted sesame seeds

Flaky sea salt, as needed

1. Preheat the oven to 350°F / 180°C. Line two baking sheets with parchment paper.

2. In a stand mixer fitted with the whisk (or in a large bowl using a hand mixer), combine the tahini, maple syrup, cornstarch, baking soda, and vanilla. Beat on medium-high speed for 4 to 5 minutes, until the batter thickens up. The batter will start very runny, but it will thicken up as you whisk.

3. Add the chopped chocolate and mix to combine.

4. Use a 3-tablespoon ice cream scoop to place the dough onto the prepared sheets. Leave 3 inches / 7.5cm of space between the cookies. Sprinkle the sesame seeds over the top. If you'd like a bakery-style look, add some more chocolate chunks to the top of each cookie.

5. Bake one sheet at a time for 15 minutes, or until the edges are golden.

6. Immediately sprinkle the cookies with a pinch of flaky sea salt. Let cool on the sheet for 5 minutes, then transfer them to a wire rack to cool completely.

7. Repeat to bake the second batch.

HEADS-UP: The kind of tahini you use really matters. It must be *thick and scoopable,* not the runny kind you can pour out like syrup. If it's too thin, the cookies will spread too much and lose their shape. The thicker the tahini, the better the cookies turn out. If your tahini is on the thinner side or you notice oil separating after beating, try adding oat flour, 1 tablespoon at a time, until you reach a thick, scoopable consistency. This helps prevent the cookies from overspreading in the oven. For the best flavor, choose a tahini made from roasted sesame seeds, not raw.

Frosted Blueberry Almond Loaf

Serves 8 — Prep: 15 minutes Cook: 55 minutes

Total: 1 hour 10 minutes, plus 1½ hours cooling time

This loaf is sure to draw attention at your next picnic, potluck, or afternoon tea. Blueberries do double duty here: Some are folded into the batter to create a gorgeous marbled texture and pockets of natural sweetness, while the rest are cooked down and whipped into a creamy frosting that's striking in its pinkish-purple hue. It's simple to make, but looks and tastes like something you'd find in a bakery window.

BLUEBERRY ALMOND LOAF

1 cup / 240ml unsweetened soy or pea milk

¾ cup / 150g granulated sugar

¼ cup / 60ml vegetable oil

¼ cup / 60g unsweetened applesauce

2 teaspoons fresh lemon juice

1 teaspoon pure vanilla extract

¼ teaspoon almond extract

1¾ cups / 235g all-purpose flour

⅔ cup / 65g almond flour

1 tablespoon cornstarch

2 teaspoons baking powder

¼ teaspoon fine sea salt

¾ cup / 115g blueberries

BLUEBERRY FROSTING

½ cup / 75g blueberries

1 tablespoon fresh lemon juice

½ cup / 115g unsalted vegan butter, at room temperature

1 cup / 130g powdered sugar

1 teaspoon pure vanilla extract

OPTIONAL DECORATIONS

Fresh blueberries

Toasted sliced almonds

1. **BAKE THE BLUEBERRY ALMOND LOAF:** Preheat the oven to 350°F / 180°C. Line an 8½ × 4½-inch / 22 × 11cm loaf pan with parchment paper.

2. In a large bowl, whisk together the milk, granulated sugar, oil, applesauce, lemon juice, vanilla, and almond extract until smooth.

3. Place a sieve over the bowl and sift in the all-purpose flour, almond flour, cornstarch, baking powder, and salt. Stir until just combined. Pour one-third of the batter into the prepared loaf pan.

4. Fold the blueberries into the remaining batter, then pour it into the pan. This helps keep the berries from sinking to the bottom during baking.

5. Bake for about 55 minutes, or until a wooden skewer inserted in the center comes out clean.

6. Let the cake cool in the pan for 10 minutes, then transfer to a wire rack to cool completely.

7. **MAKE THE BLUEBERRY FROSTING:** In a small saucepan, combine the blueberries and lemon juice and cook over medium heat for about 7 minutes, mashing the berries as they soften. Stop when the mixture thickens slightly and coats the back of a spoon—it shouldn't be too runny or too jammy. Strain the mixture into a large bowl and refrigerate until fully cooled.

8. Once chilled, use an electric mixer to beat the butter into the blueberry sauce until light and fluffy. Add the powdered sugar and vanilla and mix again until fully combined (see Heads-Up).

9. Once the cake is fully cooled, spread the frosting over the top and decorate as desired.

HEADS-UP: Depending on how much the berries reduce, the frosting might turn out a little thin—if so, just whisk in a bit more powdered sugar until it's thick enough to spread.

Upside-Down Plum Cake

Serves 8 — **Prep:** 15 minutes **Cook:** 45 minutes
Total: 1 hour, plus 20 minutes cooling time

If there's one dessert I could make over and over again without ever growing tired of it, it's this one. I only wish plums were in season all year. In this recipe, the plums are coated in a buttery brown sugar syrup that caramelizes as it bakes and soaks into the cake once it's flipped. The fruit becomes beautifully jammy and sweet, creating a stunning spiral pattern on top. It's moist, tender, and perfect with a cup of tea or coffee, and even better with a scoop of ice cream.

Vegetable oil, for the pan
2 large plums
½ cup (115g) plus 2 tablespoons unsalted vegan butter, melted
¼ cup / 55g packed light brown sugar
1¼ teaspoons ground cinnamon
¾ cup / 150g granulated sugar
½ cup / 125g unsweetened applesauce
1 teaspoon pure vanilla extract
1 cup / 135g all-purpose flour
2 teaspoons baking powder
⅛ teaspoon fine sea salt
Vegan ice cream or whipped cream (optional), for serving

1. Preheat the oven to 350°F / 180°C. Lightly grease an 8-inch / 20cm round cake pan with a bit of oil. Line the bottom with a round of parchment paper cut to fit.

2. Cut the plums in half, remove the pits, and slice them into 1/16-inch / 3mm slices.

3. Measure out 2 tablespoons of the melted butter and pour into a small bowl. Stir in the brown sugar and ¼ teaspoon of the cinnamon. Pour the mixture into the prepared pan and spread it evenly over the bottom.

4. Arrange the plum slices over the butter mixture, starting from the center and working outward in a circular pattern, slightly overlapping the slices as you go.

5. In a large bowl, whisk together the granulated sugar, the remaining ½ cup / 115g melted butter, applesauce, and vanilla until well combined.

6. Place a sieve over the bowl and sift in the flour, baking powder, the remaining 1 teaspoon cinnamon, and the salt. Gently fold into the wet ingredients, being careful not to overmix.

7. Pour the batter over the plums and spread it out evenly.

8. Bake for 40 to 45 minutes, until a toothpick inserted in the middle comes out mostly clean with just a few crumbs.

9. Let the cake cool in the pan for 20 minutes, then carefully invert it onto a cooling rack and let it cool completely.

10. Serve as is, or enjoy with a scoop of ice cream or a dollop of vegan whipped cream.

No-Bake Raspberry Coconut Cups

Serves 4

Prep: 20 minutes Cook: 0 minutes
Total: 20 minutes, plus 2 hours cooling time

When friends came over, I used to put all my energy into the main course and either grab some store-bought ice cream or skip dessert altogether. Eventually, I set out to create something that felt a bit fancy but didn't require any cooking or last-minute prep. This recipe was the result, and it's been my go-to for summer get-togethers ever since.

It's made with just two layers: a simple nut and date base that adds a gentle chew and a bit of texture, and a raspberry coconut layer that's smooth, subtly tart, and somewhere between a mousse and a cheesecake. For a simple but polished finish, I top it with fresh raspberries. If you feel like going the extra mile, add a swoosh of vegan whipped cream and a few chocolate shavings.

½ cup / 70g unsalted roasted cashews
5 Medjool dates, pitted
1 tablespoon Dutch-process cocoa powder
Pinch of fine sea salt
1 cup / 225g vegan cream cheese
⅓ cup / 80g coconut cream
⅓ cup / 80ml maple syrup
1 teaspoon pure vanilla extract
¾ cup / 90g raspberries, fresh or thawed frozen

OPTIONAL GARNISHES

Fresh raspberries
Vegan whipped cream
Chocolate shavings

1. In a small food processor, combine the cashews, dates, cocoa powder, and salt and blitz until finely ground. The mixture should hold together when pressed between your fingers.

2. Divide the mixture among 4 small glass serving cups and gently press it into the bottom. No need to pack it too tightly. Set aside.

3. In a large bowl, combine the cream cheese, coconut cream, maple syrup, and vanilla. Set a fine-mesh sieve over the bowl and use the back of a spoon to press the raspberries through the sieve so the pulp passes through and the seeds stay behind.

4. Use an electric mixer to beat everything together until smooth. (Alternatively, blend in a countertop blender.)

5. Spoon the raspberry cream into the serving cups. Refrigerate for at least 30 minutes, or 1 hour if you'd like a firmer texture.

6. Garnish as desired and dig in right away.

Cinnamon Rolls with Vanilla Coffee Frosting

Makes 9 rolls — Prep: 20 minutes Cook: 25 minutes Total: 40 minutes

Fresh cinnamon rolls without the wait. These yeast-free rolls need no rising time and are ready in under an hour. Delicious as is and even better topped with vanilla coffee frosting.

DOUGH

Vegetable oil, for the pie plate

⅔ cup / 160ml unsweetened soy or pea milk (see Heads-Up)

1 tablespoon white vinegar

2¼ cups / 305g all-purpose flour, plus more for rolling

2 tablespoons granulated sugar

2 teaspoons baking powder

½ teaspoon baking soda

½ teaspoon fine sea salt

½ cup / 110g refined coconut oil, solid

FILLING

½ cup / 46g sliced almonds or chopped pecans

½ cup / 110g packed light brown sugar

2 teaspoons ground cinnamon

2 tablespoons refined coconut oil, melted

VANILLA COFFEE FROSTING

4 teaspoons boiling water

1 tablespoon instant coffee granules

1 teaspoon pure vanilla extract

1¼ cups / 165g powdered sugar

1. Preheat the oven to 350°F / 180°C. Lightly grease a 9-inch / 23cm glass pie plate or round metal baking pan with vegetable oil.

2. MAKE THE DOUGH: In a small bowl, combine the milk and vinegar. Let sit for 5 minutes to curdle.

3. In a large bowl, mix together the flour, granulated sugar, baking powder, baking soda, and salt. Add the solid coconut oil to the flour and use forks, a pastry cutter, or your hands to press and cut until the coconut oil is in pea-size pieces and evenly distributed.

4. Pour the milk mixture into the flour and stir until a dough forms.

5. Turn the dough out onto a floured surface and knead a few times to bring it all together, adding more flour as needed to prevent sticking. Use a floured rolling pin to roll the dough into a 9 × 8-inch / 23 × 20cm rectangle.

6. MAKE THE FILLING: In a small bowl, combine the almonds, brown sugar, and cinnamon.

7. Brush the melted coconut oil over the dough rectangle. Sprinkle the filling mixture evenly all over the dough. With a long side of the rectangle facing you, use a sharp knife or a pizza cutter to cut the dough vertically into 9 strips about 1 inch / 2.5cm wide. Starting at one end of each strip, roll it up tightly to form a spiral.

8. Arrange the cinnamon rolls in the prepared pie plate.

9. Bake for 25 to 27 minutes, until golden.

10. MEANWHILE, MAKE THE FROSTING: In a medium bowl, mix the boiling water with the coffee and vanilla. Add the powdered sugar and stir until smooth. Add an extra splash of water, ½ teaspoon at a time, if a runnier texture is desired.

11. Let the rolls cool in the pie plate. Once cool, drizzle with the icing.

HEADS-UP: Soy and pea milk are recommended as they're high in protein, and this protein curdles when mixed with vinegar, helping to create vegan buttermilk.

One-Bowl Chocolate Chunk Banana Bread

FAN FAVORITE

Serves 9 — Prep: 15 minutes Cook: 55 minutes Total: 1 hour 10 minutes

This banana bread holds a special place in my heart. It was one of the first recipes I shared on the blog, and since then, it's become one of the most popular recipes on our website and the one I've made more times than any other. Whenever I have overly ripe bananas, this is the recipe I turn to. The loaf is incredibly moist, made in just one bowl, with simple ingredients you likely already have in your pantry. I'm confident it will quickly become a staple in your kitchen, just as it has in mine.

- Vegetable oil, for the pan
- 2 tablespoons ground flaxseeds
- ¼ cup / 60ml water
- 3 overly ripe bananas
- ¼ cup / 60ml vegetable oil
- ½ cup / 100g sugar
- ¼ cup / 60g unsweetened applesauce
- 1 teaspoon pure vanilla extract
- 1 teaspoon ground cinnamon
- 1 teaspoon baking soda
- ½ teaspoon baking powder
- ½ teaspoon fine sea salt
- 1¾ cups / 235g all-purpose flour
- 3.2 ounces / 90g dairy-free dark chocolate (50% to 60% cacao), coarsely chopped

1. Preheat the oven to 350°F / 180°C. Lightly grease an 8½ × 4½-inch / 22 × 11cm loaf pan with vegetable oil.

2. In a large bowl, mix the flaxseeds and water and set aside for 2 minutes to gel slightly.

3. Add the bananas to the bowl and mash well. Stir in the oil, sugar, applesauce, vanilla, cinnamon, baking soda, baking powder, and salt until well combined. Add the flour and gently mix until partly combined.

4. Set aside some of the chocolate to sprinkle on top, fold in the rest of the chocolate until just combined. Pour the batter into the prepared pan and sprinkle with the reserved chocolate.

5. Bake for about 55 minutes, or until the top is golden, the bread starts to pull away from the sides, and a toothpick inserted into the center comes out clean.

6. Allow to cool in the pan for a few minutes, then transfer to a cooling rack to cool further. Slice and serve warm.

Pecan Toffee Cookies

Makes 12 cookies — Prep: 10 minutes Cook: 25 minutes
Total: 35 minutes, plus 1 hour cooling time

You know the kind of cookie that disappears almost as soon as it hits the table? This is that cookie. Anytime I've made it, I've been asked for the recipe. They're crispy and golden at the edges, soft and chewy in the center, and studded with buttery pecans that give the cookies a toffee-like richness. Don't be surprised if they disappear fast for you, too.

BUTTERED PECANS

1 tablespoon unsalted vegan butter

1 tablespoon granulated sugar

½ cup / 50g raw pecans, chopped

COOKIE DOUGH

½ cup (1 stick / 115g) unsalted vegan butter, melted

½ cup / 110g packed light brown sugar

¼ cup / 50g granulated sugar

3 tablespoons unsweetened plant milk of choice (I use soy)

½ tablespoon pure vanilla extract

1¾ cups / 235g all-purpose flour

1½ teaspoons cornstarch

1½ teaspoons baking powder

½ teaspoon baking soda

¼ teaspoon ground cinnamon

¼ teaspoon fine sea salt

12 raw pecans (1 per cookie)

1. **MAKE THE BUTTERED PECANS:** In a small skillet, melt the butter and granulated sugar together over medium-high heat. Stir in the chopped pecans and cook for about 3 minutes, until lightly toasted and fragrant. Set aside to cool.

2. **MAKE THE COOKIE DOUGH:** In a large bowl, mix together the melted butter, brown sugar, granulated sugar, milk, and vanilla until well combined.

3. Place a sieve over the bowl and sift in the flour, cornstarch, baking powder, baking soda, cinnamon, and salt. Mix until just combined.

4. Fold in the cooled buttered pecans, then refrigerate the dough for 1 hour. (Refrigerating the dough before baking helps to firm it up, prevents excessive spreading, and enhances the texture of the final cookies.)

5. When ready to bake, preheat the oven to 350°F / 180°C. Line two baking sheets with parchment paper.

6. Use a 3-tablespoon ice cream scoop to place the dough onto the prepared sheets. Leave 2 inches / 5cm of space between the cookies. Press a single pecan on top of each cookie for a bakery-style finish.

7. Bake one sheet at a time for 13 to 15 minutes, until the edges are golden.

8. Let the cookies cool slightly on the sheet before transferring them to a wire rack to cool completely.

9. Repeat with the second batch.

HEADS-UP: In a rush and don't want to chill the dough for an hour? Just increase the flour to 2 cups / 270g and bake right away. The cookies will be a bit cakier but still deeeelish!

Chocolate Pudding
with Berry Compote & Candied Pecans

Serves 4 — Prep: 10 minutes Cook: 10 minutes
Total: 20 minutes, plus 30 minutes cooling time

In many Dutch households, a little *toetje* (a sweet treat after dinner) is almost a given. It's usually something light, like custards, puddings, or sweetened yogurts. Chocolate pudding is a classic, and my Dutch husband still gets wide-eyed and excited like a kid every time it's on the table. But store-bought versions are often not vegan, and if they are, they just don't taste quite right, so we started making our own. It comes together quickly with simple ingredients, and the toppings—candied pecans and a spoonful of stewed berries—make it feel extra special without much extra effort.

BERRY COMPOTE

1 cup / 130g frozen mixed berries

½ tablespoon sugar

CHOCOLATE PUDDING

1 ounce / 28g dairy-free dark chocolate (50% to 60% cacao), broken into pieces

2 cups / 480ml unsweetened plant milk of choice (I use soy)

⅓ cup / 65g sugar

2 tablespoons cornstarch

2 tablespoons Dutch-process cocoa powder

1 teaspoon pure vanilla extract

CANDIED PECANS

¼ cup / 25g raw pecans, chopped

1 tablespoon sugar

1. **MAKE THE BERRY COMPOTE:** In a small saucepan, combine the berries and sugar and cook at a gentle simmer over medium-high heat for about 5 minutes, or until the berries are thawed and slightly thickened. Set aside to cool.

2. **MAKE THE CHOCOLATE PUDDING:** In a medium saucepan, combine the chocolate, milk, sugar, cornstarch, cocoa powder, and vanilla. Whisk to combine and bring to a boil. Reduce the heat to medium and gently simmer, stirring constantly, for 5 minutes, or until thickened.

3. Divide the pudding among serving cups and spoon the stewed berries on top. Refrigerate for at least 30 minutes to set, or until ready to serve.

4. **MAKE THE CANDIED PECANS:** Meanwhile, in a small skillet, combine the pecans and sugar and cook over medium heat for 5 to 8 minutes, until the sugar has melted, turned an amber color, and coated the pecans. Set aside to cool.

5. To serve, top each cup with a few pieces of candied pecans.

Zucchini Muffins with Cream Cheese Frosting

Makes 12 muffins

Prep: 20 minutes Cook: 30 minutes
Total: 50 minutes, plus 40 minutes cooling time

Zucchini might not be the first thing you'd expect in muffins, but it keeps them tender and moist. The cream cheese frosting is my favorite part: deliciously sweet with pretty flecks of vanilla bean, though vanilla extract works just as well if that's what you have.

ZUCCHINI MUFFINS

- ½ cup / 120ml unsweetened soy or pea milk
- 1 tablespoon white vinegar
- Vegetable oil, for the muffin tin
- 1 small zucchini (5 ounces / 150g), coarsely grated (about 1 cup)
- ½ cup / 120ml maple syrup
- ¼ cup / 60ml vegetable oil
- 1 tablespoon pure vanilla extract
- 1½ cups / 205g all-purpose flour
- 1 teaspoon ground cinnamon
- 1 teaspoon baking powder
- ½ teaspoon baking soda
- ¼ teaspoon fine sea salt
- ¼ cup / 31g roasted walnuts (optional), finely chopped

CREAM CHEESE FROSTING

- ¼ cup / 55g vegan cream cheese
- ¼ cup (½ stick / 55g) unsalted vegan butter, at room temperature
- 1 vanilla bean, or 1 teaspoon pure vanilla extract
- 1½ cups / 195g powdered sugar
- Splash of unsweetened soy or pea milk, as needed

Candied Pecans (from Chocolate Pudding, page 253), for topping (optional)

1. **MAKE THE ZUCCHINI MUFFINS:** In a medium bowl, combine the milk and vinegar. Stir and let sit for 5 minutes to curdle.

2. Meanwhile, preheat the oven to 350°F / 180°C. Generously grease a muffin tin with vegetable oil.

3. Place the grated zucchini in a nut milk bag or clean kitchen towel and squeeze out the excess moisture. Set aside.

4. To the milk mixture, add the maple syrup, oil, and vanilla. Stir to combine.

5. In a large bowl, sift together the flour, cinnamon, baking powder, baking soda, and salt. Mix to combine. Pour the wet ingredients into the flour mixture and mix until partially combined.

6. Add the zucchini and walnuts (if using) and stir until just combined. Do not overmix. Evenly divide the batter among the muffin cups.

7. Bake for 25 to 30 minutes, until golden and a toothpick inserted comes out mostly clean with a few crumbs.

8. Let the muffins cool in the pan for a few minutes before transferring them to a wire rack to cool completely.

9. **MEANWHILE, MAKE THE CREAM CHEESE FROSTING:** In a large bowl with an electric mixer, beat the cream cheese and butter until fluffy. Split the vanilla bean lengthwise and scrape in the seeds, or add the vanilla extract. Beat until smooth. Sift in the powdered sugar and beat again until fully combined. Mix in the soy milk, 1 teaspoon at a time, as needed to achieve a spreadable frosting texture.

10. Once the muffins are cool, dollop frosting on top of each. If desired, garnish with candied pecans.

Apple Crumble Custard Tart

Serves 8

Prep: 25 minutes **Cook:** 25 minutes
Total: 50 minutes, plus 1 hour resting time

In the south of the Netherlands, no celebration is complete without a *vlaai.* It's a traditional Dutch tart, somewhat similar to an American fruit pie, but made with a soft, yeasted dough instead of a flaky crust. Vlaai is often filled with fruit or custard and sometimes finished with a lattice or crumb topping. This version is inspired by kruimelvlaai, which features a golden, buttery crumble. Inside, it's layered with smooth vanilla custard and tender apples for a dessert that feels both familiar and distinctly Dutch.

Yes, the ingredient list looks a little long, but don't be intimidated. Many of the items overlap, and overall it's surprisingly simple to make and almost impossible to mess up. The dough is soft and forgiving, and since it's meant to look rustic, there's no pressure to make it perfect.

DOUGH

- 1⅓ cups / 180g all-purpose flour
- ⅓ cup / 80ml unsweetened soy milk
- 2 tablespoons granulated sugar
- 2 tablespoons unsalted vegan butter, at room temperature
- ½ teaspoon instant yeast
- ½ teaspoon fine sea salt

APPLE FILLING

- 2 medium sweet-tart apples (12 ounces / 350g total), such as Honeycrisp, Braeburn, or Pink Lady, peeled and finely chopped
- 1 tablespoon granulated sugar
- 1 teaspoon apple cider vinegar, white vinegar, or fresh lemon juice
- 1 teaspoon ground cinnamon

1. **MAKE THE DOUGH:** In a large bowl, mix together the flour, milk, granulated sugar, butter, yeast, and salt. Knead the dough until smooth and elastic, about 5 minutes. Cover with a clean kitchen towel and let rise in a warm spot for 1 hour.

2. **MAKE THE APPLE FILLING:** In a medium bowl, mix together the apples, granulated sugar, vinegar, and cinnamon.

3. **PREPARE THE CRUMB TOPPING:** In another medium bowl, combine the flour, butter, granulated sugar, and salt. Use your hands to gently rub the butter into the mixture until it forms a crumbly texture.

4. When ready to bake, position a rack in the lowest position in the oven and preheat the oven to 400°F / 200°C.

5. **MAKE THE CUSTARD FILLING:** In a small saucepan, combine the milk, cornstarch, granulated sugar, vanilla, salt, and turmeric and whisk until smooth and lump-free. Bring to a boil over medium-high heat. Reduce the heat to a gentle simmer and cook for 3 to 4 minutes, whisking constantly.

6. Let the custard cool for about 5 minutes off the heat. It should still be warm and somewhat spreadable, not fully set.

7. **TO ASSEMBLE:** Grease a 9-inch / 23cm fluted tart pan with a removable bottom with a bit of butter. Roll out the dough into an 11-inch / 28cm round and then carefully transfer the dough to the pan. Press it in gently.

8. Use a fork to poke holes all over the bottom of the crust. If desired, sprinkle the bottom of the crust with bread crumbs–they help absorb excess moisture from the filling and keep the base from becoming soggy.

Recipe Continues

CRUMB TOPPING

1 cup / 135g all-purpose flour

⅓ cup / 75g unsalted vegan butter, cubed and chilled

⅓ cup / 65g granulated sugar

Pinch of fine sea salt

CUSTARD FILLING

1⅓ cups / 320ml unsweetened soy milk

⅓ cup / 43g cornstarch

¼ cup / 50g granulated sugar

½ tablespoon pure vanilla extract

⅛ teaspoon fine sea salt

Pinch of ground turmeric

ASSEMBLY

Softened vegan butter, for the pan

2 teaspoons bread crumbs (optional)

Powdered sugar (optional), for dusting

9. Spread the custard evenly over the bottom, layer with the apple filling, and sprinkle the crumb topping over everything.

10. Bake for 23 to 25 minutes, until the edges of the crust are golden.

11. Let the tart cool in the pan for 30 minutes before transferring to a wire rack to cool completely.

12. Slice and dust with some powdered sugar, if desired.

Nectarine & Strawberry Crisp

Serves 4 — Prep: 20 minutes Cook: 25 minutes Total: 45 minutes

When I was growing up, we had a weekend ritual. My cousins would come over for movie night, and we'd cover the living room floor with pillows and blankets. While most people enjoy popcorn with their movies, my mum made us fruit crisps. In the autumn and winter, it was always apple. But in the summer, it was some version of a stone fruit crisp.

This recipe is inspired by the memory of those nights. It's made with juicy nectarines and strawberries baked until tender and jammy. The riper the nectarines, the better, and peaches make a great substitute if that's what you've got on hand. The topping is crisp and golden, made with oats and sliced almonds for a delicious contrast. Serve it warm with a dollop of coconut yogurt or a few scoops of vegan ice cream to make it feel extra special.

- **Softened vegan butter,** for the skillet
- **3 small nectarines or peaches (about 1 pound / 455g total),** pitted and sliced
- **2 cups / 290g strawberries,** hulled and halved
- **¼ cup / 55g plus 2 tablespoons light brown sugar**
- **1½ tablespoons cornstarch**
- **1 teaspoon pure vanilla extract**
- **¾ teaspoon grated lemon zest**
- **1 teaspoon fresh lemon juice**
- **1¼ cups / 115g rolled oats**
- **⅔ cup / 65g almond flour**
- **⅔ cup / 60g sliced almonds**
- **1 teaspoon ground cinnamon**
- **½ teaspoon fine sea salt**
- **¼ teaspoon ground ginger (optional)**
- **⅓ cup / 75g unsalted vegan butter,** cubed, plus more for greasing the pan
- **Vegan vanilla ice cream or coconut yogurt,** for serving

1. Preheat the oven to 350°F / 180°C. Lightly grease a 9-inch / 23cm cast-iron skillet or round baking dish with butter.

2. In a large bowl, toss together the nectarines, strawberries, 2 tablespoons of the brown sugar, the cornstarch, vanilla, lemon zest, and lemon juice. Spread the fruit mixture evenly into the skillet.

3. In a separate bowl, mix together the oats, almond flour, sliced almonds, remaining ¼ cup / 55g brown sugar, the cinnamon, salt, and ground ginger (if using). Add the butter pieces and use your fingers to mix until the topping comes together in coarse, crumbly bits. Sprinkle the oat/almond topping evenly over the fruit.

4. Bake for 25 minutes, or until the top is golden and crispy.

5. Let cool slightly before serving. Serve with vanilla ice cream or coconut yogurt.

HEADS-UP: I used almonds here, but any nut you love, like pecans or walnuts, would work just as well.

LODGE

No-Bake Chocolate Peanut Butter Tart

Serves 10 — Prep: 20 minutes Cook: 0 minutes
Total: 20 minutes, plus 3 hours cooling time

This one's for the peanut butter lovers and anyone who appreciates a good no-bake dessert. The filling is creamy and rich, made with smooth peanut butter, thick coconut cream, and silken tofu (trust me, no one will ever guess). A small amount of espresso powder deepens the flavor, but it stays subtle. The filling isn't overly sweet, but that's by design because the cookie crust brings just the right amount of sweetness to balance it out. All in all, it takes just 20 minutes to prepare, but then comes the hardest part: waiting for it to set.

22 Oreo cookies

¼ cup / 55g refined coconut oil, melted

11 ounces / 300g silken tofu

1 cup / 255g creamy natural peanut butter

½ cup / 120g coconut cream

1 teaspoon instant espresso powder

1 teaspoon pure vanilla extract

2 ounces / 55g dairy-free dark chocolate (50% to 60% cacao), melted

Chocolate pearls or shavings (optional), for garnish

Unsalted roasted peanuts (optional), for garnish

1. Scrape out the Oreo cookie filling and place it in a bowl. Set aside.

2. Place the scraped cookies (minus their filling) in a food processor and blend into crumbs. Add the melted coconut oil and mix to combine.

3. Transfer the cookie mixture to a fluted 9-inch / 23cm round tart pan with a removable bottom and use a large spoon to press the crust down along the bottom and up the sides of the pan. Place the crust in the fridge or freezer to chill while you prepare the filling.

4. In a blender or food processor, combine the reserved cookie filling, the tofu, peanut butter, coconut cream, espresso powder, and vanilla. Blend until smooth.

5. Pour the filling into the chilled crust. Use a spatula to level the top. Refrigerate for at least 3 hours to set, but optimally overnight.

6. Decorate the tart with the melted chocolate. If desired, add chocolate pearls or shavings and roasted peanuts.

Vegan Chocolate Cake

FAN FAVORITE

Serves 12 — Prep: 20 minutes Cook: 40 minutes
Total: 1 hour, plus 45 minutes cooling time

There's no dessert more timeless and universally loved than chocolate cake, and this vegan version is one of the most popular dessert recipes from our blog (we even served it at our own wedding!). It's made with simple, everyday ingredients and comes out perfectly moist, rich, and indulgent, with a frosting that's irresistibly decadent.

CAKE

Vegetable oil, for the pans
1 cup / 240ml unsweetened soy milk
1 tablespoon white vinegar
2 cups / 270g all-purpose flour
1½ cups / 300g granulated sugar
1 cup / 95g Dutch-process cocoa
2 teaspoons baking powder
1½ teaspoons baking soda
½ teaspoon fine sea salt
¾ cup / 185g unsweetened applesauce
½ cup / 120ml brewed espresso, at room temperature
½ cup / 110g coconut oil, melted
½ tablespoon pure vanilla extract

FROSTING

1 cup (2 sticks / 225g) unsalted vegan butter, at room temperature
2¼ cups / 295g powdered sugar
¾ cup / 70g Dutch-process cocoa
⅓ cup / 80ml unsweetened soy milk
1 teaspoon pure vanilla extract
3.4 ounces / 95g dairy-free dark chocolate, melted

OPTIONAL DECORATIONS

Fresh mixed berries
Chocolate shavings

1. **MAKE THE CAKE:** Preheat the oven to 350°F / 180°C. Lightly grease two 8-inch / 20cm round cake pans with oil and line the bottoms with rounds of parchment paper cut to fit.

2. In a medium bowl, mix together the milk and vinegar. Set aside for 5 minutes to curdle, creating vegan buttermilk.

3. Place a sieve over a large bowl and sift in the flour, granulated sugar, cocoa powder, baking powder, baking soda, and salt. Mix together, then create a shallow well in the middle.

4. Returning to the medium bowl with the buttermilk, add the applesauce, espresso, melted coconut oil, and vanilla. Mix thoroughly. Add the wet ingredients to the shallow well in the dry ingredients and mix until everything is just combined, but be careful not to overmix.

5. Divide the cake batter evenly between the two prepared cake pans. Tap the pans on the counter a few times to level out the batter.

6. Bake for 35 to 40 minutes, until a thin wooden skewer inserted into the center comes out clean. Let the cakes cool in the pans for 10 minutes before transferring to a wire rack to cool completely. Be patient, as applying frosting to warm cakes can cause it to melt.

7. **MEANWHILE, MAKE THE FROSTING:** In a large bowl with an electric mixer, beat the butter until fluffy. Add the powdered sugar, cocoa powder, milk, and vanilla. Start mixing on low speed, then gradually increase to high until smooth. Once the melted chocolate has cooled slightly, mix it in.

8. Tear a piece of parchment paper into 6 squares and arrange them in a circle on a cake stand, slightly wider than the cake. This will help keep the stand clean and can be removed later.

9. Place one of the cake layers on the stand. Spread the layer with some frosting. Place the second layer on top, upside down, and frost the top and sides with the remaining frosting. Carefully remove the parchment paper squares and decorate the cake as desired.

Acknowledgments

My name might be on the cover, but if there's one thing this cookbook has taught me, it's that no one creates something like this alone. It's been a team effort from start to finish, and I feel so lucky to have been surrounded by such thoughtful, talented, and supportive people every step of the way.

Robin—my husband, my partner in business and in life. You've been here since day one, back when this was just a dream I nervously shared with you on a beach in Thailand. You believed in it before there was anything to believe in. You could've gone off to design world-saving robots, but instead you chose to help people fall in love with tofu. Honestly, your loss is the planet's gain (and to be fair, it's the tastier job anyway). Thank you for listening to my incessant ramblings, for giving me perspective when I spiraled, for rubbing my feet after a long day of cooking. You're the most incredible human I've ever met, and you are what inspires me most every day. I love you endlessly.

My little girl—you were here for every recipe test, tagging along in my belly as we chopped, stirred, styled, and photographed. You've tasted every dish (through me), and your timing for kicks was suspiciously well aligned with chocolate testing days. I can't wait to make a mess in the kitchen with you on the outside.

My parents—Mum and Dad, thank you for teaching me the value of nourishing, home-cooked meals (even if, as a kid, I insisted on eating out every other night). I didn't fully appreciate it at the time, but now I see how much that foundation shaped me. Thank you for giving me every opportunity in life, and for not freaking out when I turned down medical school to chase this wild online dream.

My sisters—Sam, thank you for opening your home to me during my uni days and letting me take over your kitchen. I didn't realize it then, but that was the spark that lit everything. You encouraged me to create, filmed my very first videos, and believed in me long before I believed in myself. And Sara, you've always been my example of strength and determination. You taught me what it means to work hard, stay grounded, and never give up. You've both lifted me up in more ways than I can count, even from across the ocean.

My in-laws—Kathleen, you've been like a second mum to me, with mine halfway across the world. You welcomed me with open arms, embraced our way of eating (and then embraced it so fully you became vegan yourself!), and became one of our biggest supporters, always cooking our recipes and sharing them with pride. And Laurens, thank you for always being willing to taste something new, even when it's a little outside your comfort zone.

Our Pick Up Limes team—Suzy Borchert, Andrea Wetzels, Sanja Prejac, María Fuentenebro, you are recipe-making, food-styling, photography-powerhouse rockstars. I couldn't have dreamt up a better group of people to build this with. Sophia Jhajj, our brilliant team dietitian, thank you for making sure everything we share is evidence-based, and for giving our readers so much confidence in the food and nutrition info we share. And Alex Nas, thank you for making our recipes look so good in video form that people had no choice but to cook them. Every day working with all of you has felt like fun, not work.

The amazing team at Clarkson Potter—thank you for believing in this project. Jennifer Sit, my wonderful editor, I'll never forget the years of encouraging nudges (aka emails) asking if I was ready. Thank you for waiting until I was. If it weren't for your persistence and confidence in me, this book would not exist. And to Stephanie Huntwork, our brilliant art director, the beautiful design of this book is thanks to your vision. Thank you for helping to bring it to life.

My agents—Kim Witherspoon and Jessica Mileo, thank you for giving me confidence as a newbie to the world of publishing. You supported my vision, stood behind me, and answered every single one of my bajillion questions.

My recipe testers—Maria Zizka and Maddie Kirkby, you are absolute gems! Thank you for testing every single recipe, catching all the little things, and for being so generous with your time and kindness. I honestly looked forward to every bit of feedback (even the parts that made me go back and retest . . . again).

My dear friends—Lieke, Patricia, Daniel, Rose, Leroy, Alex, Gaby, Imane, Cameron, Mitra, Lerin, and Cristel, thank you for always checking in, cheering me on, being my unofficial recipe testers, and for the enthusiastic oohs and aahs while eating something.

And finally, to you. To our Pick Up Limes readers and community: Thank you for tuning in, trusting our recipes, and asking for (okay, demanding) a physical cookbook. Not a day goes by that I don't feel incredibly lucky to have this "job" (and I say "job" in quotes because while yes, it's a lot of work, it's never felt like work). You've helped me find my purpose and live out my dream. Thank you, from the bottom of my heart.

Index

Note: Page references in *italics* indicate photographs.